The Little Money Book

The Little Money Book

A Field Guide to Your Financial Life

Peter Hofmann

Published by Fieldmark, LLC

ISBN: 978-1-7375189-9-0

For Maia and Nina

Contents

A Note About Resources

The Little Money Book lists resources and suggested products and services that can help you manage your finances. They are indicated in **bold type**. The suggestions reflect my own opinions. I do not get paid by any of the companies mentioned.

Direct hyperlinks to the resources are available on the book's website at **www.thelittlemoneybook.com.**

The website also contains a version of the book's text and may be updated with more current material from time to time.

Introduction

I started writing this guide for my daughters who are embarking on their own financial lives. My goal was to collect in one place advice that I failed to provide as they were growing up and that they were not learning in school. It grew into a book that I thought could help them and others become financially successful.

Let me be up-front about what the book is not. It won't make you a millionaire by age thirty. It doesn't give you a recipe for retiring at forty. It's not a pep talk or tough-love admonition. Instead, it summarizes the information I think someone trying to have a successful financial life should know. It explains important concepts and terms in simple language. It outlines steps for taking control of your finances. It lists specific financial products.

Part-way through writing the book, the COVID-19 pandemic hit. I don't know what the future holds for society, the economy, employment, and markets. Still, when it comes to personal finance, so far I see no evidence that the basic ideas I present here are wrong. Perhaps even more than before they can save you money and let you lead a more stress-free life.

How to Be Successful Thinking About Money

I'm going to push you to think about money in ways that don't come naturally.

Think long term. Money in the short term is a drug. It's a dopamine fix when you have it and an anxiety attack when you don't. But money in the long term is an ally. It puts goals and aspirations within reach and reduces stress and unhappiness.

Think "times." When you think long term, money behaves unexpectedly. With money you don't add, you multiply changes over many periods. It's surprising what happens when you multiply inflation rates or investment returns over many years.

Look beyond "average." A lot of what you read and hear about money is true on average. But you are not average. Your situation, your starting point, and your goals are unique to you.

Accept uncertainty. Money decisions are invariably about the future, but the future is unknown. There are no guarantees. You can try to put the odds in your favor, but always realize you can get lucky...or unlucky.

Be skeptical. The financial industry is huge and sophisticated. It uses fear and greed to trick you into buying expensive products and services you don't need. Always ask how much something will cost and how the person or company you are dealing with gets paid.

Chapter 1:What is Money?

George Bailey: "Only one way you can help me. You don't happen to have eight thousand bucks on you?"

Clarence (his guardian angel): "Oh, no, no. We don't use money in Heaven."

George Bailey: "Oh, that's right, I keep forgetting. Comes in pretty handy down here, bub."

– It's a Wonderful Life (1946)

Down here, we need money. We need it to eat, to pay for a roof over our head, to buy clothing, medicines, concert tickets, and pretty much anything else we need or want. Once upon a time, we might have been able to barter, trade our stuff for other stuff, our services for those of others. These days, for most things we'll just take money, thank you.

But what exactly *is* money? The dollar bill in your pocket? Your checking account balance? What about an iTunes gift card? The IOU from your roommate? The weird Australian gold coin your uncle gave you on your first birthday?

For one, money is a *unit of measurement*—an agreed way of measuring prices, like Fahrenheit and Centigrade scales are agreed ways of measuring temperatures. Different countries use different units, or currencies. In the U.S., we've agreed to use the dollar as the accepted method. Much of Europe uses the *euro*, Mexico the *peso*, China the *renminbi* (also called the "yuan.") McDonalds will sell you a Big Mac meal for $5.67 in the U.S., but in Mexico you will pay about 50 pesos. Meanwhile, in China the average price is 21.50 yuan. We can't really compare these unless we convert them all into one currency, which is what *The Economist* magazine does when it calculates the cost of a Big Mac around the world converted into U.S. dollars.

U.S. $ Price of a Big Mac

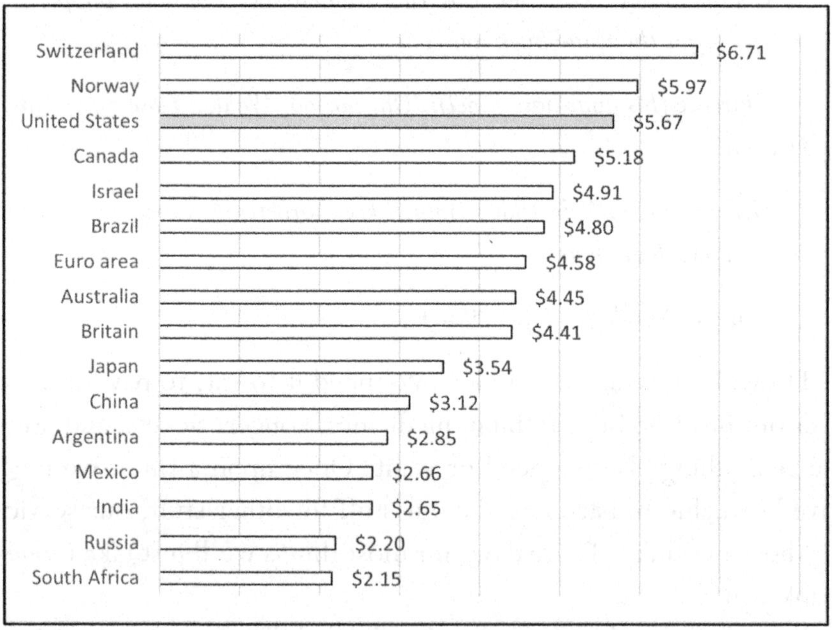

Data source: *The Economist*, January 2020

But money is more than that. Once we've agreed how to measure prices, money is a *medium of exchange*. With money, I can be confident that I'll be able to buy and sell anything rather than having to barter. Its value is known, and it is readily and widely accepted.

We also want to be able to buy and sell in the future at similar prices as today. In other words, we want money to be a good *store of value*. If I have to work fifteen minutes at my job to make $5.67 today to buy myself a Big Mac, I don't want to go to McDonalds next week and find out that a Big Mac now costs $6.67. I don't want to worry about the value of my money going down too much in the future.

Most of the time the value of money—measured in terms of what stuff costs—indeed goes down (meaning the prices of things go up). This is inflation. Inflation recently has been pretty low in the United States: less than 2% a year. If you have a dollar and hang on to it, in a year it will only buy you what 98 cents buys you today. "Big deal," you say, "I can live with that."

It wasn't ever thus. In 1980, inflation in the U.S. reached almost 15%. In one year, a dollar dropped in value to 87. Throughout history and around the world inflation has at times hit extremes, making money useless as a store of value. As of this writing in October 2019, for example, inflation in Argentina is 53%. People are standing in line at banks to change their pesos into U.S. dollars as quickly as possible because they are losing value so fast.

What assurances do we have that the dollar is a good store of value? Basically, we've put our faith in the government to make sure that inflation doesn't get out of hand. Our central bank, the Federal Reserve (a.k.a "the Fed") is charged with this job. They have been shooting to keep inflation right around 2% a year. Despite lots of huffing and puffing by politicians and armchair central bankers, they've been doing a pretty good job.[1]

Here's the thing, though. Over time even 2% inflation steadily erodes the value of money. In ten years, a dollar only buys 82 cents worth of stuff. In forty years, that's down to 45 cents. This is why sticking your money under the mattress is a bad idea. You need to do

---

[1] There is debate about how low inflation should go. People get worried when inflation approaches zero percent. While it's good when products get cheaper because of competition and greater productivity, most economists don't want *overall* prices in the economy to decrease. This is deflation, the most severe example of which was during the Great Depression. Nobody wants a repeat of the Great Depression.

something with it to make sure your savings at least keep up with inflation.

Should you really worry about *forty* years from now? Absolutely! Read on.

Are Cryptocurrencies Money?

Cryptocurrencies—such as Bitcoin and Ethereum—are becoming more mainstream. Their prices have gone through major ups and downs but have generally increased. Gradually a financial ecosystem is growing up around them, and it looks like they may be here to stay. How should we think about these new kids on the money block?

Let's take Bitcoin, the most popular cryptocurrency. On the one hand, it is just a bunch of electronic entries in a ledger, not unlike most money in circulation. The difference is that it is not controlled by a central government. The government does not determine the amount of bitcoin in circulation. It won't let you pay your taxes in bitcoin. It doesn't issue bonds denominated in Bitcoin.

The jury is out on whether Bitcoin will ever stand side by side with centrally managed currencies such as the dollar. So far, it flunks the test: as a *unit of measurement,* it hasn't made the cut. People still by and large set prices in traditional currencies, even if they then convert them into Bitcoin. As a *medium of exchange,* it can be used in some stores, in virtual settings, and for various illicit activities; but has not become generally accepted, let alone "legal," tender. And as a *store of value,* it remains incredibly unreliable because of how much its price jumps around.

For now, think of Bitcoin and other cryptocurrencies as speculative investments. We don't know whether any of them will be like gold—which has remained valuable over millennia and across civilizations—or a blip in digital history. As with any risky bet, some people have gotten fabulously wealthy by buying crypto, while many others have lost a lot of money. Bottom line: don't buy any with cash that you cannot afford to lose.

Chapter 2: Money for a Lifetime

Larry Garfield: "You want to play the game? Learn to play it right."

Kate Sullivan: "Oh, is that what you call it, a 'game?'"

Larry Garfield: "You're damn right. The best game in the world. I'll teach you. It's easy. You make as much as you can for as long as you can."

Kate Sullivan: "And then what?"

Larry Garfield: "And then what? Whoever has the most when he dies, wins. Look. It's the American way."

– Other People's Money (1991)

For a few unlucky souls like Larry "the Liquidator" Garfield, money is the purpose of life. The rest of us just want to make sure we have *enough*. "Enough" is not a number. It is the ability to live the life we want. Some people make do with very little. Some people are in the 1% and don't have to worry. For the rest of us, it's about how much money we have coming in and how we manage our expectations of "enough."

When we are young, our money lies ahead of us—in the form of future earnings. Those potential earnings depend on a lot of factors, many not in our control, including (unfortunately) gender, race, social networks, and the economy, but also intelligence, skills, career choices, education, and health. The wonky term for this is *human capital*. The thing to remember about your human capital is that it is a *finite amount*.

Here's some simplified math. A "typical" working lifetime may span forty-five years. This means that somebody making on average $60,000 a year can expect lifetime earnings of perhaps $2.7 million. That $2.7 million has to pay not just for living expenses while working, but also for retirement, which could be another thirty years. Over the long arc of a lifetime, then, the challenge is figuring out how to make $2.7 million last for seventy-five years. Simple math tells us we have $36,000 a year available. That's on average how much this "typical" person can support, before we get into such fun topics as saving and investing.

Annual Income	Number of Future Working Years	Total Future Earnings, Plus Money Already Saved	Future Working Years Plus Retirement Years	Available per Year
$60,000	45	$2,700,000	75	$36,000

I encourage you to repeat this simple formula with your own aspirations. Count only *future* years and add any savings you've already accumulated. Just dreaming? The Bureau of Labor Statistics has data on how much various professions pay at **www.bls.gov/oes**.

So how do you accomplish this "spreading" of money over a lifetime? The short answer: you save.

Before you leave the room in disgust, sneering, "I can't save 40% of my pay,"[2] hear me out. First of all, you can expect to collect some Social Security when you retire, as long as you pay taxes into the system (more on that later). In addition, the earlier you start saving,

---

[2] Spend $36,000 out of $60,000, save the difference: $24,000/$60,000 = 40%

the more *investment income* you get, thanks to the power of compounding (more on that later, too). By the time you factor these in, saving about 15% of your pay for retirement will get the job done.

We will come back to the important questions of how much to save, how to save, and how to invest the money you save. But first, we need to earn us some money.

Chapter 3: Money at Work

Sgt. Sean Dignam: "I'm the guy who does his job. You must be the other guy."

– The Departed (2006)

It's good and well—and important—to theorize about human capital. But the rubber hits the road when we go out and get a job. Work is how most of us get our money. It's how we turn earnings *potential* into *income*.

Anatomy of a Paycheck

Money from work will come in one of two basic forms: wages from an employer or income as a self-employed person (e.g., as an independent contractor, sole proprietor of a business, or consultant). Shown below is what a typical pay statement from an employer might look like.

Let's go line by line. If you have a pay statement, take it out and compare. You may not have all these items, or you may have some others.

Gross pay is pretty straightforward. If your salary is $60,000 a year and you get paid twice a month your gross pay will be, as in this example, $2,500. Then there are a number of *deductions*.

Before anything else, your employer withholds *Social Security tax* (part of what's known as *FICA taxes*). This tax is actually 12.4% of gross pay, of which the employer pays half and you pay the other half. This tax pays for the Social Security benefits of people who are retired today. It does not get tucked away in some "trust fund" for you, which is a common misconception.[3] *Your* benefits will be paid for by people who are working when *you* are retired. Social Security is what's known as a "pay-as-you-go" pension system.

A Typical Paycheck

Earnings	
Gross Pay	$2,500.00
Statutory Deductions	
Social Security Tax	-$155.00
Medicare Tax	-$36.25
Federal Income Tax	-$277.08
State Income Tax	-$115.45
Pre-Tax Deductions	
Health Insurance	-$41.00
401 (k)	-$50.00
HSA / FSA	-$100.00
After-Tax Deductions	
Roth 401 (k)	-$50.00
LTD	-$9.00
Net Pay	$1,666.22
Taxable Wages	$2,309.00

The next item, *Medicare tax* (the other part of FICA) is 2.9% of gross pay and works the same way, except it pays for Medicare benefits. Medicare is health insurance provided by the government to anyone over the age of sixty-five. Again, you pay half and your

[3] The Social Security "trust fund" people talk about is extra money that was built up when FICA taxes collected were more than the benefits being paid to retirees. Today more money is going out than coming in and the fund is shrinking.

employer pays half. By the way, don't confuse Medicare with *Medicaid*, which is medical insurance provided by your state if you're poor.

Next are *income taxes* that your employer withholds and pays to the government. Unlike Social Security and Medicare taxes which are deducted at a set rate, the income taxes withheld are an estimate. This estimate is based on the **Form W-4** that you fill out. When you file your tax return (by April 15 of the following year), the tax withheld during the year is either more or less than you owe. You either get a refund or pay the difference. State taxes (and in some places local/city taxes) work the same way.

Income taxes are calculated using your taxable wages, which is your gross income minus the *pre-tax deductions* we'll discuss next. So more pre-tax deductions mean lower taxes.

If you get health insurance through work you will likely have a deduction for the insurance premiums. Many employers pick up a significant chunk of this cost. Your pay statement only shows the part that you pay.

Another benefit that some employers offer is the opportunity to put some "pre-tax" money into a *Health Savings Account (HSA)* or a *Flexible Spending Account (FSA)*. We'll cover these accounts in later chapters.

If your employer offers a *defined contribution retirement plan*—such as a 401(k) or 403(b) plan—you can put money into the plan and invest it for retirement. This is a great opportunity because the money can grow and no taxes are due until you withdraw it many years later. It's an even greater opportunity if your employer *matches* your contribution. For example, a plan could specify that the employer contributes 0.5% for every 1% of your pay you contribute, up to 6%. In that example, you receive 3% extra compensation, without having to pay taxes on it until years down the road. You end up with 9% of your pay stashed away for retirement.

You may also have some *after-tax deductions*. These could be for a variety of benefits. I've given two examples in the table.

Some retirement plans offer a *"Roth"* option (named after a former U.S. Senator from Delaware). As with the regular 401(k) contribution, you specify how much you want contributed to a Roth account. While you contribute money that you have already paid taxes on, the beauty of a Roth contribution is that you get to invest the money and never pay any tax when you ultimately withdraw it.

Another example of an after-tax deduction is *long-term disability insurance (LTD)*. This is insurance that pays you if you cannot work. It is often a voluntary benefit; if it is offered, I strongly recommend you get it. Some employers give you the option of having the premium withheld after tax. *Do this*. Typically it is not a lot of money and the benefit will be tax-free should you become disabled. Be aware that this insurance may not go with you if you switch jobs.

After all the deductions are taken out of your gross pay, you are left with the *net pay* you take home.

Self-Employment

We live in the gig economy, so many folks are self-employed. For independent contractors, business owners, consultants, and the like, keeping track of money is more complicated. If you make more than $400 in a year, you owe taxes. Nobody will be withholding them from your pay, so you need make quarterly tax payments to the Internal Revenue Service (IRS) and maybe your state tax department. You're effectively running a business, which means you'll need to keep a record of money coming in and expenses going out. With receipts to prove it.

You will also have to cover some of the costs that an employer would otherwise pick up. That means paying the entire 15.3% of FICA taxes on your income (both the employer and employee shares). It means paying 100% of your health insurance premiums. And it means that you need to figure out your own retirement plan. On the plus side, you get a tax break on many of these expenses, so it's not quite as severe as it sounds.

If you get paid in cash you're still required to report the income and pay taxes on it. What if you don't? Well for one, you are breaking the law. Further, when you work "under the table" for too long, you get dinged when it comes to receiving Social Security and Medicare, both of which require that you pay FICA taxes for at least ten years.

None of this is meant to discourage anyone from being their own boss. Just be aware that the financial responsibilities that come with being self-employed are greater than when working for an employer.

Chapter 4: Money in the Bank

Stanley Ipkiss: "How about that account? We have... checking, savings and checking, CDs, savings and CDs, checking and CDs, savings, checking, and CDs, T-bills, or we can just take all your money and throw it in a big mattress back there."

– The Mask (1994)

Opening a bank account is one of the first steps into the jungle called "financial services." Beware! There are lots of predators, large and small, looking for a piece of your fleece. They come with friendly faces, alluring offers, breathless promises, and a lot of fine print. But the mattress is not an option. So grit your teeth and take the plunge.

To start, it helps to know that banks make money off you in two basic ways—one you see, the other you don't. The one you see consists of a laundry list of *fees* for various things. The other is called the *spread*. When you put money in the bank, the bank turns around and invests it. They earn more from lending out or investing your money than they pay you in interest. The difference is what is known as the "spread." The more money you deposit, the more spread they get to keep.

For example, when you open a checking account, you may see an "account maintenance" fee, but the bank may agree to waive that fee if you keep a certain balance in the account. They get paid either way.

Of course, banks are businesses that deserve to earn a profit so they can provide their services. It's up to you to keep them honest by shopping around. Luckily the banking business is incredibly competitive, so you can find good deals.

Two Accounts You Need

I suggest everyone have at least two bank accounts:

A *checking account* that *charges few fees* to be used for day-to-day transactions—accepting paychecks, making deposits, and paying bills. These days almost all checking accounts come with a debit card that you can use to access your money to pay for things in stores and online.

A *savings account* that *pays a high interest rate*, often advertised as "high-yield savings" or "high-yield money market" accounts. It doesn't need to be at the same bank as the checking account[4], but the two should be electronically linked (a one-time process) so money can be transferred back and forth. Some banks let you open several savings accounts so you can create different savings "buckets" for various goals.

Choosing a bank is boring and there's a temptation to go with the first one you see. But comparison shopping on the web is easy thanks to sites such as **Nerdwallet.com**, **Bankrate.com**, and **Depositaccounts.com**. Think about how much time you put into comparison shopping for all the "stuff" in your life (you know...shoes, fishing rods, organic yarns, etc.) Commit at least as much time to comparing bank accounts. It will save you thousands of dollars over the years. If you are one of

[4] Many banks almost automatically give you a savings account when you open a checking account. You don't need to use this account if it doesn't pay a high interest rate. It's okay to open another savings account somewhere else that does.

those "average" Americans who has had the same checking account for sixteen years and pays $14 per month in fees, this goes for you too.[5]

When it comes to choosing a checking account, think about what is most important to you. Here are some considerations:

- Are there ATMs that will be free to use near your home, work, or where you shop? Check the "in-network" ATM locator for the bank you're considering.
- Do you want to do your banking in person so you can ask questions and get to know the people? A branch nearby, perhaps at a local bank or credit union, might fit the bill.
- Do you expect to travel a lot, including internationally? A mega bank with nationwide coverage and extra services could be for you.
- Do you live, breathe, and sleep online? A pure internet bank may be just right.
- Are you a foreign national living in the U.S. or regularly send money overseas? There are accounts that cater to people who don't have Social Security numbers. One example is **Passbook**.
- Do you need to write checks? Personally, I find it convenient every now and then, but with some "checking" accounts actual checks are no longer an option.

For savings accounts, look for a high interest rate. Interest rates can change daily, so make sure to compare the most current ones. The best rates are often paid by purely online banks. Do some research. Sometimes you can find sign-on bonuses in the hundreds of dollars.

A natural question when thinking about opening any kind of bank account is: How safe is my money? Luckily, there are strong protections in place today; the federal government guarantees that if a bank goes belly up you won't lose the money in your account. Specifically, accounts are insured up to $250,000 by either the Federal

---

[5] Amanda Dixon, "Our Long, Long, Long Relationships With Banks: Are We Missing Out On Better Deals?", Bankrate.com,10/23/2017

Deposit Insurance Corporation (FDIC) or National Credit Union Administration (NCUA). As long as your account is protected by one of these two, you're good.

Apps That Zap

Once you have a checking account, you can connect *payment apps* to it that let you easily send money to anyone using just their email or phone number. **Venmo**, **Zelle**, **Cash-App**, and **PayPal** are among the most popular—super convenient and fast. But watch out: once you've sent money with one of these apps it may be impossible to get it back if you change your mind.

Also, these so-called "fintech" companies often are not banks, so your money may not be protected by the FDIC. Some will deposit your money in an insured bank account; in that case, check the fine print to see which bank.

Juicing Up Savings

Another kind of federally guaranteed savings account you can get at a bank is a *certificate of deposit (CD)*. Usually you earn higher interest rates with CDs than ordinary savings accounts because they require that you put the money in for a longer period (between three months and five years is typical). Certificates of deposit are very easy to open at a bank where you already have an account because the bank has all your necessary personal information. If you're sure you won't need the money for some set period, CDs are a very safe way to earn extra interest. Pay attention though, because most CDs renew automatically. You will need to tell the bank if you want the money to go back into your regular savings or checking account at the end of the term.

The Credit Score You've Never Heard Of

You've been turned down trying to open a checking account. Life happens, and perhaps you've gone through some financial ups and downs. If you've had accounts in the past, it's possible that you have a low ChexSystems score, which reflects incidents of bounced checks, insufficient funds, or fraudulent activity. You can get your score and report free once a year at **chexsystems.com**. If you are rejected, don't despair. It takes five years for your record to clear; in the meantime, there are other banking options from companies such as **GreenDot** and **Chime**.

Resources

Government and Regulatory Agencies		
FDIC BankFind	Search all FDIC-insured banks	**https://banks.data.fdic.gov/bankfind-suite/bankfind**

Chapter 5: Living with Money

Alberta Marlow: "I'm not so obsessed with money as you seem to be. I can do without it."

Rick Leland: "You stick around with me and you'll get plenty of practice."

– Across the Pacific (1942)

It's time to dig into the messy business of figuring out how to live with what you got, moneywise. There is no single right way to do this. The trick is to find a way you can stick with and that fits your personality. If you're a real planner and list-maker, you might have the discipline to track every penny coming in and going out. If not, you should at least establish some guardrails to keep from careening into a mountain of debt and crashing your financial future.

Try this five-step approach. Pencil and paper required.

Step 1: Get the Lay of the Land

Your mission is to prepare two financial statements that are key to understanding your financial situation. The first is your personal *cashflow statement*, which lays out how much money you make and spend in a month. The second is your personal *balance sheet*, which measures your wealth.

If you have never done this, do it today. In the future, repeat it if things seem to be going off course and in particular *before* you make major financial decisions such as signing a lease, making a large purchase, making a life change such as moving or having a child, or taking out *any* loan (student loan, car loan, mortgage, personal loan).

The Cashflow Statement

Start by writing down all money you have coming in every month (or expect to be coming in if you are starting a new job). Include your net pay, side-hustles, business profits, child support—any source. If your pay is very variable, try to figure out a conservative monthly average. *Add* to this any contributions to retirement or savings plans withheld from your paychecks.

For money going out, I like a method described by Elizabeth Warren and her daughter Amelia Warren Tyagi [6], which creates three buckets: "must-haves," "wants," and "savings."

"Must-haves" are the big bills you *have* to pay for necessities:

- taxes (if not withheld by an employer)
- housing (rent or mortgage plus home maintenance)
- utilities
- essential groceries
- childcare
- health and other insurance
- transportation
- minimum debt payments (student loans, car loans, credit cards)

For bills that come quarterly or annually, estimate a monthly average.

Now add up how much goes to savings each month. Savings includes retirement contributions made by your employer, any money you put aside for future use, and any change in your debt

---

[6] Elizabeth Warren and Amelia Warren Tyagi, *All Your Worth: The Ultimate Lifetime Money Plan*, Simon & Schuster Inc., New York 2005.

balances. Think of debt as negative savings: if the balance goes down, add the *change* to savings; if the balance goes up, subtract it.

Here comes the magic. Subtract the "must-haves" and the savings from the money coming in and you have the money you can spend on "wants:"

Money in – Must Haves – Savings = Wants

If you keep track of these four big things there is no need to write down every movie ticket, chai latte, or pair of jeans you spend your "wants" money on.

The next page has an example of a cashflow statement, using some of the numbers from the sample pay statement. (Recall that we assumed each month consists of two pay periods.)

Take stock. What fraction of the money coming in goes to these essential expenses? Warren and Tyagi recommend a simple *50-30-20 Rule* that says you shouldn't spend more than about 50% of the money you have coming in each month on "must-haves." You can spend 30% on "wants," and you should try to save 20%. These numbers aren't hard and fast, but they represent a balanced goal that will allow you avoid a lot of money anxiety. If you are way off the mark, it's time to adjust. Warren and Tyagi's book, while a little out-of-date, gives some practical pointers on how to approach difficult choices if they are necessary. In our example, "must-have" expenses of 73% are high compared with the guideline and may require some tough choices. To achieve the 50% goal, "must-have" expenses would need to be lowered by $868. This would allow more savings and more spending on "wants."

Sample Cashflow Statement

Money In		
Take-home pay	$3,244	
Lyft driving (net of expenses)	$150	
401 (k)contributions withheld	$200	
HSA contributions withheld	$200	
Total Money In	**$3,794**	**100%**
"Must-Have" Expenses		
Est. taxes on Lyft income	-$40	
Rent	-$1,400	
Utilities (electric, heat, water)	-$200	
Essential groceries	-$400	
Student loans	-$300	
Credit card Payment	-50	
Auto loan payment	-$250	
Auto (gas, insurance, service)	-$125	
Health insurance	Withheld by employer	
Total "Must-Have" Expenses	**$2,765**	**73%**
Savings		
401 (k) contributions	$200	
HSA contributions	$200	
Savings account additions	$300	
Increase in credit card balance	-$200	
Total Savings	**$500**	**13%**
"Wants" Expenses		
Total "Wants" Expenses	**$529**	**14%**

The Balance Sheet

The second financial statement you should prepare every now and then is a household balance sheet. It's important because it focuses on both your *assets* and *liabilities*. Your wealth is measured by your *net worth*, which is the difference between the two. The goal is to increase net worth over time by increasing assets and reducing debt. Here is an example:

Sample Balance Sheet

Assets		Liabilities	
Checking Account	$400	Student Loan	$27,000
Savings Account	$2,550	Auto Loan	$5,000
Investments	$12,000	Credit Card	$800
Primary Residence	$280,000	Mortgage	$242,000
Total Assets	**$294,950**	**Total Liabilities**	**$274,800**
		Net Worth	**$20,150**

A balance sheet is always as of a point in time. Refer to your account statements and write down outstanding *balances*, not payment amounts. To estimate a value of a home, you can use market values used for property tax calculations or develop your own estimate with some research. Real estate sites such as **zillow.com** will often show estimates of value, or you can look up values for similar homes that were sold in the previous two years or so.

Step 2: Set Goals

By now you should have clear picture of your financial situation. The next step is to write down your goals. Try to be specific both in terms of the timeframe and the amounts involved. Having clear, specific goals is a foundation of a lot of planning. Goals should be in order of priority, and usually go short-term to long-term. For example:

- Save an emergency fund of $1,000
- Contribute to a 401(k) up to any employer match
- Eliminate credit card debt and auto debt in twelve months

- Pay off college loans in five years
- Save $40,000 for down payment on a condo

Your goals should be individual to you, but they should reflect the following priorities:

Emergency fund: You should be able to handle an unexpected expense without adding to debt. There is no hard and fast rule as to how big such a fund should be but start with $500 to $1,500 as an initial goal. This should be the minimum balance in your savings account. Try to build it to two and ultimately six months of expenses over time to handle bigger unexpected events such as a job loss or medical emergency. If you find yourself dipping into it every month, it's not an "emergency" fund. Use it rarely, and make sure to replenish it after you do.

Retirement fund: If you have a 401(k) or 403(b) plan at work, make sure to contribute at least the amount needed to maximize any matching contribution from your employer. The match is compensation that your employer expects to pay you, so be sure to take it. There are also reasons to set a higher target which we'll cover in the chapter on retirement.

Pay down debt: We will cover debt in detail in another chapter; in general, you should try to pay down as much as possible as quickly as possible, starting with the highest interest debt.

Beyond these general priorities, save for the big things that are important to you. Being explicit about how much you are trying to accumulate can be daunting, but as you begin to progress toward your goal, it can keep you motivated.

So go figure out your goals. Write them down. Stick 'em on the fridge (okay, maybe not).

Step 3: Adjust

You've faced your financial reality and set goals. If your spending is in balance and you have positive net worth, you may not need to adjust much. If your "must-have" spending is around 50% and you are saving 20% you are in good shape, unless you set very aggressive goals that require you to significantly increase your savings. If your spending is out of balance, or you have significant negative net worth you may need to consider changes in your living situation and maybe even your job(s). You should, of course, be prudent about spending on "wants," but pinching pennies at the corner coffee shop isn't going to pay off your student loans. It is the large changes that have the most dramatic impact.

Step 4: Automate Spending and Saving

When it comes to money, we can be our own worst enemies. Temptations are everywhere, and the "math" we do in our heads is often completely off base. One way to fight these impulses is to automate spending and saving, taking some money "out of sight, out of mind." Here are some tips:

- Make sure to set up contributions to retirement plans from each paycheck
- Have part of your paycheck deposited directly into your savings account
- Set up automatic payments for recurring bills on paydays

Step 5: Create a Budget

Once you have a cashflow statement in hand it's time make a *budget*. What's a budget? It's a plan for spending *in the future*. Take your cashflow statement and for each major category write down how much you expect to earn, save, and spend next month. Try to plan for at least three months, or, if you're feeling ambitious, for a whole year.

Writing down a budget forces you to be specific about the amounts you plan to spend and allows you to compare your actual spending to your plan. It's a commitment to yourself to keep on track. If you end up spending more than planned in one area, compensate by spending less in another or in the following month.

Budgeting is a chore that falls by the wayside despite the best of intentions. Newbies need to build new habits and discipline. It doesn't much matter how you do it, as long as you find a way to stick with it.

One very low-tech approach is to literally use separate envelopes in which you put cash for different purposes for the next month: for food, for gas, for entertainment, etc. This allows you to ration your money in a very physical and direct way.

When you don't use cash, you need another way. You can write everything down in a notebook. You can use one of many **spreadsheets** available for free (or build your own). Or you can use a budgeting app, of which there are a many. Some are free, others charge between $40 and $130 a year. One of the largest is **Mint**, owned by personal finance behemoth Intuit. It's free, but you agree to share personal information and subject yourself to marketing pitches. **You Need a Budget** (YNAB) is a well-regarded paid option. There are many others. Check out the latest reviews on **Nerdwallet**.

With many of these apps you can connect to your bank, credit card, and investment accounts and automatically update your balances, pay your bills, and categorize your spending. To take advantage of these capabilities, you need to share usernames and passwords with the apps. This is a risk, but if it helps you save and control your spending the risk may be worth it.

Another important consideration is whether you are budgeting just for yourself or for a household that includes others. Some apps are designed to sync easily across devices and allow more than one person to enter information.

Glib Advice

If you read about personal finance, it won't be long until you come upon such pearls of wisdom as "spend less than you make." Duh! Yes, there are situations where crazy spending habits and other poor decisions, such as buying too much house, too much car, or running up credit card balances, are the culprits. Financial planning can help with these. There are also situations where life has dealt finances a blow (for example a job loss, illness, or injury) and the numbers don't work anymore. Planning and learning about money can be part of the solution. But for many people the problem is simply insufficient income. There are no budgeting strategies or investing silver bullets that will make you rich trying to support a family on a minimum wage job. "Financial literacy" is no cure for poverty. Still, understanding the concepts in this book is worthwhile, because unfortunately it's often when people are struggling that they are most vulnerable to financial missteps and rip-offs.

Chapter 6: Money Around Town

*Tyler Durden: "You are not your job. You're not how much money you have in the bank. You're not the car you drive. You're not the contents of your wallet. You're not your f*** khakis. You're the all-singing, all-dancing crap of the world."*

– Fight Club (1999)

Spending money is wrapped up in a lot of emotion. We don't want to get ripped off. We don't want to seem cheap. We want to brag about deals. We want to show off luxuries. We feel superior because we spend more than others. We feel superior because of how frugal we are. Those losers in coach. Those idiots in first class. Pride and envy, always jostling for the top spot.

I'm not your shrink, but I encourage you to keep some perspective and be smart about your spending. Regardless of your income, there's more stuff to be had every day, more temptations to which to succumb, more "bucket list" experiences on which to blow your money.

But here is a simple truth: if you want to reach your savings goals faster, spend less. It's up to you to draw the line. In that spirit, here are three pointers to keep your spending in check.

Check lifestyle creep. As your income (hopefully) increases so does the urge to splurge: more expensive cars, homes, vacations. But it can be more subtle. In your twenties, you launder and iron your own shirts. In your thirties, you drop them at the cleaners. In your forties, you buy them by the dozen and open a new one when you need it. In your fifties, you're hand-tailored all the way. Go back to spending like you're in your twenties.

Consider buying used (or last year's model). Cars lose 60% of their value in the first five years. Last year's fashion sells at 50% off—even more if slightly used at a thrift shop.

Negotiate everything. Ask for the employee discount; the cash discount; the "old age" discount; the "good customer" discount; the Wednesday, Thursday, Friday...you get the point. It never hurts to ask. And arm yourself with information. Research and comparison shopping are easily done on the web.

How to Pay for Stuff

Remember the role of money as a "medium of exchange?" This is where we talk about some tips, tricks, and pitfalls when paying for things day to day.

Cash

Cash has the great benefit that you can't spend more than you have. For people who tend to be a little loose with money, cash helps control spending impulses.

Cash can get you discounts. Some businesses post separate, lower prices for cash. Those that don't may still give them—*if you ask.* You might be surprised how much you can save even on larger transactions, such as car repairs.

Cash transactions are anonymous, if you care about that kind of thing. The flipside to anonymity is security. There is some risk of loss or theft when carrying around a wad of bills.

Cash also makes it harder to track your spending. You need to save receipts or make a note of purchases, whereas with cards you have statements to which to refer.

If you like cash, you'll want access to ATMs that don't charge any fees for withdrawals. Make sure the machine you use is in your bank's network.

The ability to pay with cash is becoming more limited. Some large transactions may not be feasible, and even some smaller purchases—such as in-flight purchases on major airlines—must be made with cards.

Checks

Checks are a risky form of payment, and unless a business requires it there is little reason to use them. Avoid carrying around checks since your account number and other personal details are printed on them. Also, to avoid hefty returned-check fees, make sure that there are funds in your account when the check is cashed. Sometimes this can be weeks or months later when you've forgotten about it.

Debit Cards

Debit cards are a lot like cash. They hit your bank account immediately. If you have not signed up for overdraft protection, transactions will be rejected if you don't have enough money in your account. You know right away, and there is no fee.

For businesses that offer a lower cash price, that price will sometimes be honored for debit cards.

Most debit cards are processed through one of the major payment networks: Visa, Mastercard, Discover, or American Express. This means that any store that accepts these cards should honor your debit card.

If you need to contest a fraudulent charge, debit cards can be a hassle, depending on the bank. By law, they can require you to contact them within two days. Wait longer, and you could lose up to $500.[7] Then you have to wait for the money to go back into your account. If

[7] 12 CFR § 205.6 - Liability of consumer for unauthorized transfers, Cornell Law School Legal Information Institute

you have the option, avoid using debit cards in situations where you might need to dispute a charge if things don't turn out as expected. Examples are online orders, deposits on big purchases or travel, and recurring payments (such as gym memberships where charges might continue even if you cancel).

Credit Cards

Credit cards are a huge double-edged sword. They are great for payments, but terrible if you carry a balance. To take advantage of the benefits, always pay off your entire credit card balance by the due date.

When you use a credit card, merchants pay a percentage of the amount to the credit card company; 1.5% to 4% is typical. They are willing to do this because it allows them to have more sales. Some businesses, notably gas stations, explicitly charge higher prices for credit card transactions.

Many credit cards give you airline miles, loyalty points, or money back on purchases. You can trade in these points for deals on airfares or hotel rooms.[8] *But...don't let the point tail wag the purchase dog.* Getting 3% cash back on a $100 purchase that you wouldn't have otherwise made means you're $97 poorer.

A big benefit of credit cards is they protect you against unauthorized transactions. You're not responsible for charges you didn't approve. Credit card companies are getting very good at spotting and alerting you to suspicious transactions and will let you instantly block the card against further use.

You are also covered if something you bought with a credit card is defective or not as described. The first step should always be to try and work things out with the seller. But if you can't, contact the bank

---

[8] Travel and credit card points are big business. Check out https://thepointsguy.com/ for some of the latest deals.

and dispute the transaction. They will reverse the charge and handle the dispute with the merchant.

Gift or Reward Cards

These cards (or apps) are a little like cash, but not really. Let's use one of the biggest, Starbucks Rewards, as an example. You put money on the card. Then you get a free coffee for every $25 you spend. If you're a Starbucks junkie and keep the balance low (say, under $25) this can be a good deal. But if you keep a high balance or don't go often, it's not. You're just letting Starbucks use your money. And if you want to cash out, you can't—except in chai lattes. Still, people have $1.6 billion (that's billion with a "b") stored on Starbucks cards.[9]

Another reason not to have big balances on gift cards is that if the business goes belly up there's a good chance you will lose whatever amount is still on the card.

If you do opt for these cards, be sure to either use the app or register your card so you can recover its value if it's lost or stolen.

Your Smartphone (or Watch)

Money has moved onto your devices. A variety of apps can be linked to one or more of your credit cards, debit cards, or bank accounts and used to make or receive payments. Some of these apps store balances, others just move money in and out of your accounts. Its best to keep any balances small. You don't earn any interest on them, and they may not be insured by the FDIC the way bank accounts are.

Apple Pay, **Google Pay**, and **Samsung Pay** are among the largest of these *digital wallets*. Each lets you make contactless payments at merchants that accept them. Digital wallets are a good way to use credit or debit cards. Transactions are very secure because they don't reveal your card numbers.

---

[9] JP Koning, "Starbucks: Monetary Superpower", blogpost, 8/21/2019

To send money to—or better yet, receive money from—individuals you can use one of an ever-increasing number of *peer-to-peer payment apps*, including **Apple Cash**, **PayPal**, **Venmo**, **Cash-App**, **Zelle**, and **Facebook Pay**. They offer convenience and low cost. However, check twice before pressing "SEND". There is no "JK" button to take back a payment.

Chapter 7: Other People's Money?

Rub Squeers: "Can I borrow a dollar?"

Sully: "Nope. You can borrow a jelly doughnut, though."

Rub Squeers: "You can't borrow a jelly doughnut. Once you eat it, it's gone."

Sully: "Once you borrow a dollar, it's gone. I'd rather buy you a jelly doughnut."

– Nobody's Fool (1994)

We are constantly tempted to borrow: credit card offers, home-equity loans, zero-percent financing, layaway offers, don't-pay-until-next-year deals, easy overdraft protection, payday loans, accelerated tax refunds, rent-to-own deals...the list goes on. What do these have in common? They are all debt.

Wall Street has a saying that debt is "other people's money." Wrong! Every dollar you borrow is a dollar *you* have to pay back. Debt is money borrowed *from your future self* that you are spending today.

Recall our discussion of human capital from Chapter 2: *your lifetime earnings are finite*. In our simple example there was $36,000 to spend each year. What happens if you take out a five-year car loan for $20,000 at "zero percent financing?" You only have $32,000 left to spend in the following five years because you've "pre-spent" $4,000 a year.

I could fill the page with numbers about the crushing debt load on American households from student loans, credit card debt, car loans, personal loans, medical debt, and many others. I'm not going to. You already know whether you are part of these statistics. If you are, getting out of debt should be a key goal for you.

Debt Basics

Debt is such an important topic that we need to get a little technical. First let's define some terms:

- A *loan* is money borrowed, usually for a fixed period. Mortgages, student loans, and car loans are examples of loans. A *line of credit*, also known as a *revolving credit line*, is an amount that you have *available* to borrow, up to a limit. Credit cards, home equity lines of credit (HELOCs), bank overdraft protection are lines of credit. Once you borrow from a line of credit you have a loan.
- *Principal* is the amount borrowed. With most debt you pay a little bit of principal back with each payment. This is called *amortization*. Sometimes you pay all the principal at the end in a single "balloon" payment.
- *Interest* is an amount you pay for the privilege of borrowing. It's common to make monthly payments of interest and some principal amortization. Interest is calculated by multiplying an *interest rate* times the amount of principal outstanding at the beginning of the month. The interest rate is often expressed as an "annual percentage rate" or *APR*. For monthly payments you divide this rate by twelve.
- *Fixed rate* debt has one interest rate for the entire term of the loan. With *adjustable* or *floating rate* debt the interest rate can change periodically.

- *Secured debt* is debt backed or "secured" by an asset. The asset is known as *collateral*. For example, a *mortgage* is debt secured by real estate, like your house. If you miss payments, the lender can foreclose (take your house). Auto loans are backed by a car. The lender can repossess ("repo") the car if you fail to pay.
- *Unsecured debt* is only backed by your promise to repay. Lenders can come after you for repayment, but they can't just take your stuff. The interest rate on unsecured debt generally is much higher than on secured debt.
- *Co-signers* are people who sign the loan documents and agree to pay if the borrower doesn't. They are on the hook just as much as a borrower. *Do not co-sign a loan lightly*, and not at all if you don't have the money to repay the debt.

Interest rates change all the time. Here are some typical rates (APRs) as I'm writing this:

Type of Loan	APR[10]
30-Year Fixed-Rate Mortgage	3.88%
15-Year Fixed-Rate Mortgage	3.22%
5-Year Adjustable-Rate Mortgage (ARM)	3.28%
48-Month New Car Loan	4.56%
Federal Undergraduate Student Loans	4.53%
Federal Graduate Student Loans	6.08%
Credit Card	17.55%
Credit Card Penalty Rate	29.99%
Payday Loan (borrow $200, pay back $235 in two weeks)	458.86%

[10] Data sources (as of 10/30/2019): The Wall Street Journal, U.S. Department of Education, Bankrate.com, Lendup.com

Debt Mind-Games

Banks and other retailers play mental tricks to get you to borrow. Here are some to watch out for.

Size-of-Payment Ploys

One of the most common ploys lenders use is to focus on the size of the payment. This is a terrible way to look at debt. Here is how it works. A car dealer will ask you, "How much can you afford a month?" They'll offer you a four-year, $10,000 loan with a 5% APR, which will cost you $230.30 a month. You balk. "Too much? How about I save you $40 bucks a month and make the payment $188.71? We'll just make it a five-year loan. Sign here..."

You see what happened there? Multiply the payments times the number of months. With the four-year loan you pay back $11,054; with the five-year loan $11,323. Instead of "saving you $40 bucks a month" the dealer *made* an extra $269. *Always know the total you have to pay back, including interest.* This should be disclosed. If it isn't, ask.

Another size-of-payment trick is the "minimum payment" on credit card bills. This is how lenders get around talking about ridiculously high interest rates. Here is an example from an actual recent credit card bill. The statement balance was $1,990. The minimum payment the bank wanted was $35. "No problem. I can afford $35. This isn't so bad."

But the bill also includes this (required) disclosure: "*If you make no additional charges using this card and each month you pay only the minimum payment you will pay off the balance shown on this statement in about **8 years** and you will end up paying an estimated total of **$3,579**.*" Do the math. The bank makes $1,589 for lending me $1,990! That's what happens with an APR of 17.24% (which I had to find in the small print at the end of the statement). *Always know your APR.*

Things get downright criminal with very short-term loans, such as the payday loan example in the table. You "only" pay $35 to get $200 to tide you over for two weeks. Then here is what happens. You get your next paycheck and pay back $235. But because you just repaid the loan, you're short again. Borrow another $200, and the cycle repeats. After a year, you will have paid $972 in interest because of a *one-time need* to borrow $200. That's called a "debt trap," and it's why payday loans are illegal in many states.

During grad school, I had a job at a little shop in Brooklyn that was always in a cash crunch. Every Friday night, "Tony" would stop by after closing to collect his cash. I wonder whether he did as well as these payday lenders.

Discount Hooks

Ever go into a store to buy something and have the cashier offer a big discount right then and there if you sign up for a store credit card? It can be hard to resist these "hooks." But once you have signed up, the retailer has won. You are now more likely to direct some of your dollars to this store, especially when you start getting a barrage of "member sales" and "special deals." It also makes it easy to run up debt balances. If you succumb to many of these offers, it becomes harder and harder to keep track of total debt because it is all broken up across balances on many different store cards.

Zero Percent Offers

It gets uglier. Be careful when a store or credit card tempts you with "zero percent" financing. These are often "deferred interest" offers, which require you to pay off the balance within a certain time period. Which is fine *if* you meet the deadline. But in real life, stuff happens. Perhaps you don't have the money one month or just forget to make a payment. If that happens, you risk being charged a sky-high interest rate *retroactively*. Example: you buy a $1,000 washer on a twelve-month, 0% deferred interest offer. You diligently pay $83 a month but forget to make one payment on time. All of a sudden, instead of 0% you're charged 29.99% interest and owe an extra $140 on your washer.[11]

Another ploy by credit card companies is to tempt you with "0% balance transfers." They want you to switch cards and move your debt to them. Dig a bit deeper into these offers and you find that you'll be charged 3% or more just to make the transfer. If you have a balance where you are paying a high APR this may actually be a good deal, but it is not zero.

You can "game" these offers to your advantage, but the companies have figured out that many people will be confused, forgetful, or too financially stretched to pull it off. If you decide to play this game, be very diligent and understand the details in the fine print.

Debt to Avoid

Credit Cards

The ideal credit card discussion is short: *pay off the entire statement balance by the due date every month*. Every month. Every card. Fini. Do this, and the APR on the card doesn't matter. You will not owe any interest. Instead, you get to use the bank's money for free from the date of each charge to the due date on the statement. But miss the due date by one day or pay one dollar less than the statement balance and you owe interest starting the date of the charge. Plus a hefty late charge for any payments past the due date.

Credit cards are, therefore, a boon to people who charge only what they can pay off, but poison for those who carry a balance or forget to make payments on time.

If you have arranged your spending according to the 50-30-20 rule (see Chapter 5 for a refresher), you are much more likely to be in the

---

[11] Gail Hillebrand, "How to Understand Special Promotional Financing Offers on Credit Cards", Consumer Financial Protection Bureau, 6/8/2017

first group. You can use your card strategically to pay bills and accumulate reward points without ever paying a finance charge.

If you're in the second group, you need to make changes. Some of these may sound silly, but you have to find a way to not use the card at all or pay it off.

- Stop carrying the card
- Don't "auto-pay" any bills from the card (substitute your debit card)
- Put the card in a place where it is difficult to access
- Remove the card from any sites where it is saved as a payment method (e.g., Amazon)
- Disconnect the card from mobile wallets and payment apps

Debt to Buy a (New) Car

Buying a car is a significant financial commitment. Go ahead and drool over Ecoboost turbocharged engines and Moonlight Blue Metallic paint. But also crunch some numbers. Most importantly, take time to reflect what is important to you. Then keep in mind the following.

One: buying a *new* car is *a dumb financial move*. The average new car loses 60% of its value in five years.[12] That means a $30,000 car will be worth $11,700 after five years. Still people do it. I've done it myself. I'm a car guy…I get it. But it's not worth digging yourself into a financial hole for.

Two: Buying used saves you money. A new car will be a used car immediately when you drive it off the lot. If you want a newer model, buy one that is a year or two old and save thousands.

Three: Spend time figuring out how much car you can afford. Go back to the 50-30-20 rule and figure out your transportation budget.

If you don't *need* a car, consider using public transportation, biking, or other alternatives. Use short-term rentals such as Zipcar for when

[12] Rick Popely, Car Depreciation and How Much it Costs You, Carfax.com, 2/3/2021

you want to get out of town on weekends. Be like a European. It's sexy and you'll save a lot of money.

If you absolutely need a car, crunch the numbers. Your car payment plus all the other costs of ownership should fit in the 50% "must-have" spending bucket. Estimate how many miles you'll drive a year and the cost of gas for different models. Get quotes from insurance companies, research reliability data, and get typical repair costs for the cars you are considering. Then look at your budget. For example, say your transportation budget is 10%. In our earlier example, that comes to roughly $400. Say half of that goes to insurance, gas, etc. That leaves $200 a month to pay for the actual car.

Four: Don't take out a car loan for more than thirty-six months. Five, six, and even seven-year loans are increasingly common, and they are a trap.[13] The longer the loan, the greater the risk of having "negative equity" in your car, i.e., owing more on the loan than the car is worth. These are "size of payment" ploys designed to make you buy more car than you can afford. Also, if you don't think you want a used car today, what makes you think you'll want one in three years. Your new car will be three years old, and you'll still owe two to four years on your loan.

Back to our example... If you have $200 a month available for thirty-six months, you can afford a car costing about $6,700. This is not unreasonable—very solid used cars can be had for this amount and even less. The best way to achieve this is to save up that amount and pay cash. But even if you have to borrow some, it is now a reasonable debt.

Five and finally: Leasing is debt. When you lease a car, you commit to making monthly payments from your future income. And at the end, you own nothing. You return the car to the dealer. It's another "size of payment" game: the payments can be lower because you only

---

[13] Ben Eisen and Adrienne Roberts, "The Seven-Year Auto Loan: America's Middle Class Can't Afford Its Cars", The Wall Street Journal, 10/1/2019

pay to *use* a car for some years. (Basically, you are paying for the depreciation of the car while you use it.) That said, leasing may be right for you if want to permanently devote a portion of your monthly budget to car payments and drive a new one every few years. Make sure your lease term is shorter than the warranty on the car so you're not on the hook for any major repairs.[14]

[14] For more on the pros and cons of leasing see Consumer Reports, "Leasing vs Buying a New Car", www.consumerreports.org/buying-a-car/leasing-vs-buying-a-new-car

Chapter 8: Money from Later

Jack Walsh: "How much is here?"

Jonathan Mardukas: "Neighborhood of three hundred thousand."

Jack Walsh: "That's a, that's a... very respectable neighborhood."

– Midnight Run (1988)

It may surprise you at this point that I don't think all debt is bad. Debt can be useful. Again, back to our human capital example: your lifetime earnings are a finite amount. When you borrow, you use some of your future earnings today. For this privilege you pay a higher price (through interest payments). When does this make sense? It can make sense if what you buy goes up in value (appreciates) rather than down (depreciates). It can make sense if what you buy increases your future earnings. It can make sense when there is no alternative. And it can make sense when you want to spend money on an opportunity that might not come by again.

Buying a Home

Owning their own home is one of the biggest goals for many people. Plunking down cash for a place is out of reach for most, so this is one instance where borrowing is the only option. If you're fortunate, a house will also increase in value. But a lot depends on your specific situation, and it's rarely a financial slam-dunk. Here we're going to just focus on some features of mortgages that are important to understand.

Say we have a $300,000 home in our sights. Nowadays, some first-time homeowners can make a down payment of as little as 3%. Pay just $9,000 and borrow $291,000. (There would also be several thousand more in *closing costs*: attorneys, appraisals, taxes, title insurance and such.)

Home equity is the amount of the house that is included in your net worth: the value of the home minus the outstanding mortgage balance. At the beginning, equity is equal to the down payment, in this case, $9,000.

Let's look at a 30-year mortgage with an APR of 3.88% (from our earlier table). The mortgage payment in this case comes to just over $1,369 a month. For the first payment, $941 of this will be interest.[15] The remaining $428 will reduce the loan balance, so equity increases to $9,428. Every month, equity increases a little more, slower at the beginning, faster later on, until it the loan is paid off. After five years, assuming the house has the same value, equity is $37,311, an increase of $28,311.

The upper graph on the next page shows what the path over thirty years looks like if the home value stays the same. In reality, home equity changes as you pay off the loan but also as the value of the home changes. The lower graph shows the path for a hypothetical home whose value changed with average home prices from 1990 to 2020. Home prices increased nicely overall, but there was a period of five years between 2006 and 2011 where they fell. It took another five years to get back to the level of 2006. Home price appreciation is not guaranteed.

[15] Remember, interest is the balance times the APR/12, in this case $291,000 x 0.0388/12 = $941

Mortgage Pay-Off Path

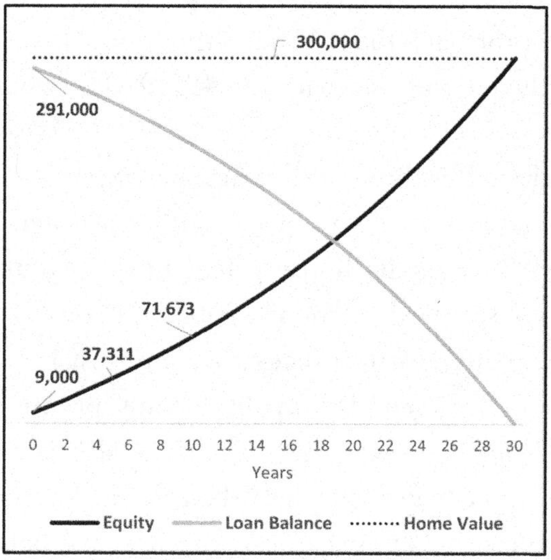

Mortgage Pay-Off Path With Changing Home Value[16]

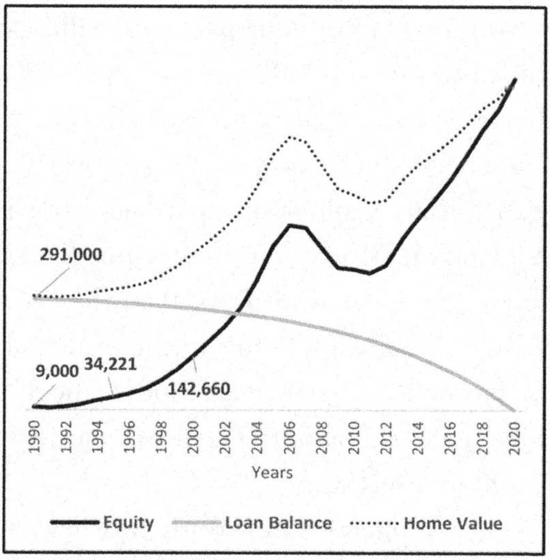

---

[16] This assumes a mortgage with the average APR in 1990, which was 10.31%. Price changes are based on the yearly average S&P/Case Shiller National Home Price Index. Data from the Federal Reserve Bank of St. Louis.

Reducing Interest Cost

Back to our mortgage loan. What's the total you have to pay back? Adding up all the payments comes to $492,920, of which $201,920 is interest.

You can reduce this interest cost in four ways:

1. *Borrow less.* Banks used to require a down payment of at least 20% of the house price. In our example, if you put down $60,000 (20% of $300,000) and borrow $240,000 the smaller loan reduces total interest paid by more than $35,000. You also avoid paying premiums for *private mortgage insurance* every month, which is usually required for down payments less than 20%. Borrowing less may require saving for a few extra years before taking the plunge on a home purchase.
2. *Choose a shorter term.* The rate on a 15-year mortgage is usually lower than on a 30-year mortgage. With the 3.22% rate from our table, your payment will be higher ($2,041 in this case) but you will save over $125,000 in interest.
3. *Pay more than the required payment.* Even if you can't afford the higher payment of a 15-year mortgage, always make sure that you are allowed to pay back your mortgage faster than planned. Mortgages should not have any *prepayment penalties.* If you send in more than the required payment, banks will usually apply this to the principal. For example, if you pay an extra $100 each month, the 30-year mortgage will be paid off about 3½ years earlier and save over $27,000 in interest.
4. *Find a lower interest rate.* With mortgages, even a small difference in the APR can make a big difference. In our example, finding an APR just a quarter of a percent lower saves $15,000 in interest. A mortgage is the kind of big

decision for which doing research and negotiating make a difference.

Ready to borrow? As you shop around for a good rate you may find yourself talking to different types of companies that arrange for or "originate" mortgages. These include *mortgage bankers*, *mortgage lenders,* or *mortgage brokers,* among others. Lenders and bankers put up the money to lend to you; brokers are middlemen who work for a fee representing several lenders. Always remember that these companies do not work for you. They get paid more if you borrow more, which means they may try to focus just on the size of the payment and push you toward a larger loan. When shopping around, compare local bank and broker interest rates with online services such as Bankrate.com. Always focus on the APR of the loan which will include any up-front interest charges known as *points.* One point is equal to 1% of the loan paid up front.

Once your mortgage is in place, you may interact with a different *mortgage servicer* than the bank who made the loan. It is not unusual for a mortgage to switch servicers several times over its lifetime, but this will not affect the payments you owe.

Going to College

With crazy-high tuition costs, does it even still make sense to go? Most researchers who have looked at the issue have concluded yes.[17] The overarching reason is that you can expect significantly higher income with a college degree. Taking on some debt to afford college

[17] See for example Jason R. Abel and Richard Deitz, "Do the Benefits of College Still Outweigh the Costs?" Federal Reserve Bank of New York, Current Issues in Economics and Finance, Volume 20, Number 3, 2014.

can make sense, but take on too much and the advantage may disappear.[18]

While this is *generally* true it may or may not be true *for you*. Just because somebody is willing to lend you money does not mean you should take it. The degree you pursue matters. So does your age, the income you can expect after graduation, and the earnings you give up while in school.

Student loans get pretty complicated. Do your research, starting with the government's website at **https://studentaid.ed.gov/sa/**. Here are a few important points to keep in mind.

Student loans fall into two general categories: federal and private.[19] With federal debt you are borrowing from the government, whereas with private loans you are borrowing from a bank.

How much is safe to borrow? There's no single right answer, but a common guideline is not to exceed the annual income you expect to earn after graduation. That's in the $45,000 to $60,000 range for most undergraduates, which will take $475 to $640 a month for ten years to pay back at a 5% APR. If you already have other debt, that needs to be factored in. A large debt load can affect all aspects of life. People with more student debt tend to wait longer to marry or buy a home and they tend to be more likely to take a job outside their chosen field.[20]

Standard federal student loans are paid back over ten years. At a 4.53% interest rate for undergraduates, for every $10,000 you borrow you pay back a total of approximately $12,453. As with all debt, you save interest if you can pay back the loan more quickly.

---

[18] William R. Emmons, Ana H. Kent and Lowell R. Ricketts, "Is College Still Worth It? The New Calculus of Falling Returns", Center for Household Financial Stability, Federal Reserve Bank of St. Louis, 1/7/2019.

[19] A number of states have student loan programs as well.

[20] Mark Kantrowitz, "Student Loan Debt Causes Delays in Achieving Major Financial Goals", SavingForCollege.com, 6/28/2019

A benefit of federal student loans is that they allow a variety of repayment plans. These plans can stretch out your payments or lower your payments early on but will cost more overall than the 10-year plan. Also, if you are having trouble repaying federal loans, you may be able to temporarily stop making payments. This is known as *forbearance*. It's important to understand that if you are approved for forbearance *your loan balance will increase* by the amount of interest you did not pay. It may be better to opt for an income-driven repayment plan, which means that, if your income is low, you may have a *zero* required payment without adding more interest to your loan.[21]

There are some risks to dealing with the government. It's a giant bureaucracy and there is nobody you can appeal to. Miss a loan payment and risk joining the one-in-ten borrowers who are *delinquent* on their payments. Worse, you could end up in *default* of a loan. Default has a number of consequences, all of them bad.[22] Ultimately, if you don't pay up, the government will garnish you wages. And I don't mean garnish with parsley, I mean literally remove the money from your bank account. With the government, you owe debt until you pay it off or until it is forgiven.

Private student loans require even more vigilance. Now you are dealing with lenders who want to make money off you. Your first question should be: Why do I need a private loan? If the answer is because you've reached the limit on federal loans, think carefully before proceeding and adding to your debt burden. Also, it's critical to read the loan documents carefully and understand all the major provisions, which can differ a lot from one bank to another. Ask for help if you don't.

---

[21] Kimberly Rodgers Cornaggia and Han Xia, "Who Mismanages Student Loans and Why?", August 21, 2020. Available at SSRN: https://ssrn.com/abstract=3686937

[22] Cheryl Winokur Munk, "What to Know About Missing a Student-Loan Payment", The Wall Street Journal, 10/3/2019

Family Matters

When it comes to student debt, family finances almost always come into play. It's natural for parents to want to help their children go to college, and the system pushes them to do it. Federal Parent PLUS loans are specifically designed for parents to help pay their kids' college expenses. They are easy to get and, unlike loans taken out by students, have no set maximum amount that can be borrowed. When it comes to private loans, lenders often require parents as co-signers to get the best rates.

The upshot is that parents can end up with a lot of their children's student debt—often more than the students themselves. Parents end up saving less, with potential implications for their own financial security. An open conversation about the family's financial resources can put everyone on the same page, even if it is difficult to broach the subject.

Dealing with an Emergency

Sometimes we borrow because we have to—a medical emergency, a relative in need, a major home repair. Faced with an emergency we should be clear-eyed and say: I am prepared to sacrifice my future income for this.

If you have to borrow for an emergency, look for the lowest interest rate. You may be tempted by the convenience of a credit card, but it is an expensive convenience. Explore other options. For medical bills contact the provider and negotiate (see Chapter 23 for more tips). For larger acquisitions or repairs, see if you can spread out the payments. Remember, money is money (it's *fungible)*. You can try to negotiate payments on *other* bills, for example by talking to your mortgage servicer or utility company, and then use the freed-up money toward the emergency expense. If you have a 401(k), you can consider borrowing from it (see box). Perhaps borrowing from family or a friend are an option, but be sensitive to the impact owing money can have on relationships.

My Precious

Debt can be okay when a) you can afford to make the payments and b) you have made a clear-eyed decision to sacrifice future income for something special today. What qualifies? That is up to the individual. Say you are an avid mountain climber and want to splurge on a Himalayan climbing expedition. Go ahead. If you wait and save until you can pay cash you may miss the opportunity. Or maybe you're an aspiring actor and have an opportunity to audition for an excellent movie part. Go ahead and borrow to pay the airfare.

This advice is a little dangerous. Instant gratification is a big draw. For example, I'd suggest that borrowing to go on a luxury vacation doesn't make sense, even if though it may give you some pleasure. Ask yourself, "Can I still get this or do this in x months or years if I save up the money." If the answer is yes, save up and postpone the satisfaction. It will be all the sweeter when you can pay cash.

The point is, borrowing thoughtfully and with a clear commitment to subsequently tighten your belt until the debt is paid off, can absolutely work. Unfortunately, it's all too easy to tell ourselves that we will be disciplined and then fail to follow through. That's where we get into trouble.

Refinancing

Say you have a student loan or a mortgage with a fixed interest rate. You notice that interest rates on new loans are now much lower. Someone taking out a loan today is getting a better deal than you did. This situation has become common, because since the 1980s there has been a steady downward trend in interest rates. No surprise then that it has become common for borrowers to *refinance* their debt—i.e., take out a new loan to pay off the old one and get the lower interest rate.

30-Year Mortgage Fixed Rate

Data Source: Federal Reserve Bank of St. Louis

How do you know whether refinancing makes sense?

The answer depends on individual circumstances. It is easy to get tricked into thinking you are saving money just because you can reduce your monthly loan payments. Lenders push "savings" from lower payments very aggressively because they make money each time you take out a new loan. But not so fast. Often a big part of the lower payment is from extending the debt (recall the "size of payment ploy" from the previous chapter). You can end up with a lower monthly payment and still pay more interest over time because you pay for longer.

The only way to figure out whether to refinance is to crunch some numbers. There are a lot of moving parts, so the answer is not always clear. You can access a **worksheet** through this book's website that lets you try out different scenarios.

Refinancing a mortgage often involves new closing costs (fees for attorneys, taxes, and the like). That means the savings from a lower interest rate must be at least large enough for long enough to cover those costs.

Refinancing is most likely to be beneficial if one or more of the following is true:

- You have a large remaining balance; interest savings on a smaller balance may not be significant enough.
- You plan to keep the home for several more years; if you sell in a year or two the monthly savings won't add up to much.
- The new interest rate is least 1% lower than your current rate.
- You can eliminate the cost of private mortgage insurance (PMI) because the home has increased in value.
- Your credit score has improved a lot.
- You have an adjustable-rate mortgage and would like to lock in a low fixed rate.

It can be tempting to do a "cash-out" mortgage refinancing—one where you take out a larger loan than your current balance without increasing your monthly payment. This is the size-of-payment ploy working in the other direction. By extending your loan and paying a lower interest rate you can borrow more. Look at a cash-out refinancing as two loans: (1) The first refinances your existing mortgage balance; this makes sense if you can save on interest. (2) The other is entirely new debt. Whether this makes sense depends on what you do with the money.

If you are thinking of refinancing your student loans, be sure to do your homework. Federal loans can only be refinanced with private loans and it is a one-way street. Once you have moved to private loans there is no way back; you lose the flexibility of federal loans or access to any relief that the government might make available. (Federal loan **consolidation** is not refinancing and doesn't save you any money.)

Borrowing From Your 401(k)

Most 401(k) plans allow you to take a "loan" of up to half your account balance. This can make sense if you are borrowing for a good reason. The best way to think of it is as a temporary withdrawal of your retirement funds. You commit to putting the money back with some extra to cover the "interest," usually over up to five years (longer if you are using the money to buy a home).

But there are caveats. First, the money you take out is no longer working for you earning investment income. You are short-changing your retirement kitty. This matters most if you're shooting for high returns with your retirement funds, usually by investing in stocks. Second, if you leave your job before the loan is repaid, the rest will be due by the time you file your next tax return. If you've become unemployed you probably don't need this extra cash crunch. Third, you run the risk of developing a bad habit.

Chapter 9: Money Trap

Agent Rick Dicker: "You want to get out of the hole? First you're going to have to put down the shovel."

– Incredibles 2 (2018)

Debt is a like a drug. Start using it, and the debt cartel (banks) starts pushing more and more offers on you. Each deal comes with an enticement. Each payment seems small and manageable. Before you know it, you have thirteen charge cards, tapped into overdraft protection on your checking account, taken out a home equity loan and two car loans. Oh, and you're still paying off your student loans and mortgage. You've stolen every penny from your future earnings to keep you head above water. The whole thing is at risk of tumbling down.

Before you reach that precarious state, make a point of getting out. There are no easy or quick ways to accomplish this, except the earlier you start the sooner it will be done. Sit down, face the problem, work out the numbers, and start chipping away at it.

A Step-by-Step "Get out of Debt" Plan

This plan is the *economically* most effective: you pay down the highest cost debt as quickly as possible. You may see other plans that focus on *psychological* "wins", like paying off small debt balances first even if they have lower interest rates. At the end of the day what is most important is to have a plan that you stick to.

Step 1: List All Your Debts

Make a list of all your debts as follows:

Card/Loan Name	Credit Limit	Balance	Rate (APR)	Minimum Payment	Due Date	Planned Payment

If your credit is good, or you have equity in your home, you can consider consolidating your debt into a single loan to lower your interest payments. Before you do, make sure you know how you ended up here and test your commitment to becoming debt-free. The last thing you want is to add to your debt.

Step 2: Plan Monthly Payments

Add up your minimum payments. Make sure these are *paid on time*. Now pull funds from other spending buckets. Cut your "Wants" spending to the bone for a few months. Stop all saving (except enough 401(k) contributions to get any employer match). Drain your savings accounts (except for an emergency balance). Pull money out of investments if you have them. Use every available penny to make additional payments, starting with the highest APR balances and working your way down ("planned payments" in the chart). Do this every month until the only debts you have left are student loans, mortgages, and car notes with interest rates less than 4%. **Unbury.me** is a calculator that can help you keep track.

Step 3: Change Your Incentives

Once these debts are paid off, *stop using all but one credit card*, preferably the oldest. Hide or even destroy the others. Close those accounts gradually over time, starting with the newest, to minimize the impact on your credit score. Also close any card accounts that charge annual fees. Make the card you keep difficult to access, as described above, but use it occasionally for some small recurring expenditures.

Pay for everything else with either a debit card or cash.

If you have overdraft protection on your checking account, have it removed. Make sure that your bank will reject debit transactions that are more than the balance in your checking account.

Freeze your credit (instructions later). By freezing your credit, you block inquiries to your credit report, which will keep you from being approved for instant credit offers and reduce the number of mail solicitations.

Strive to go back to saving 20% of your incoming money. This will be a lot easier once you no longer have interest payments on debt to contend with.

Last Recourse

Sometimes nothing works. A situation is so dire that there is no obvious way out. It's time to seek help. There is no shame in this, and it's not the end of the world. The details are beyond this book, but one avenue to consider is a *debt management program*. These combine debts into a single monthly payment that pays everything off over three to five years. Counselors who put these programs together work for non-profit organizations. This doesn't mean they work for free; they may charge a fee and are also paid by the debtors.

It's best to avoid *debt settlement* or *debt relief* companies who ask for monthly payments and then haggle with creditors with no guarantee that the debts will be paid off. It may be better to look into filing for bankruptcy and get about rebuilding quickly.

Credit Scores

The original purpose of credit scores was to for lenders to determine whether it was safe to lend you money and how much interest to charge. A higher score got you more credit and lower interest rates. But credit scores are creeping into other walks of life. Landlords check them before renting a place to you. Insurance companies are using them to figure how high a premium to charge you. And employers are increasingly reviewing them as part of vetting job candidates.

It is not surprising then that anxiety over credit scores has increased. Just remember that credit scores don't judge you as a person. They don't reflect your moral character. They are a statistical assessment of whether you have had credit and how you have managed it. Also remember that a high credit score should not be treated as a license to pile on debt.

There are three major *credit bureaus*, **Experian**, **Equifax**, and **Transunion**, that continuously collect information on your outstanding debt, credit card balances, and payment history. If you are late or delinquent in paying a bill, lenders and merchants report it to the credit bureaus.

Before approving you for a loan or line of credit, a lender will check your credit score. There are many different credit scores; the most widely used ones are calculated by Fair Isaac Corporation and are known as *FICO scores*.

FICO scores range from 350 to 850[23]:

FICO Score	Creditworthiness
800 or higher	Exceptional
740 – 799	Very Good
670 – 739	Good
580 – 669	Fair
579 or lower	Poor

[23] All credit score data from myFico.com, accessed 5/11/2021

Your credit scores will determine how much you can borrow and the interest rate you have to pay. Here are some typical recent rates for a 36-month auto loan:

FICO Score	Rate for 36-Month Auto Loan
720-850	3.8%
690-719	5.1%
660-689	7.5%
620-659	10.4%
590-619	14.9%
500-589	16.3%

How are FICO scores calculated? The exact formula isn't public, but here are the major factors that go into the mix:

Factor	Weight
Payment History	35%
Amounts Owed	30%
Length of Credit History	15%
Credit Mix	10%
Recent Searches for New Credit	10%

The bizarre thing is that everyone wants to sell you *your* credit score! Fair Isaac does. It can be hard to find out your score without paying up. In addition to Fair Isaac, each of the three credit bureaus also calculate credit scores, and unless the information they have on you differs, these scores will probably be similar. There is no need to worry about differences of a few points between different scores. Also, some credit bureaus have begun to make scores available for free, as have some banks and credit card companies. And if you're not squeamish about giving up your personal information and being bombarded with solicitations, credit monitoring sites such as

CreditKarma or **WalletHub.com** will also provide you with scores for free. (Full disclosure: I'm squeamish.)

The credit reports that underlie the scores detail your past and present debt and payment record. You are entitled to receive a credit report from each of the three bureaus once a year for free. The easiest way is to go to **www.annualcreditreport.com**. You should do this and check the reports for accuracy. You can contest incorrect information and have it removed. One approach is to request one of the three reports every four months, which lets you review each bureau on a twelve-month cycle. Since the COVID-19 pandemic, all three credit bureaus have been offering *weekly* free credit reports. They may or may not continue doing this.

How to Get a High Credit Score

If you have a low credit score either because you haven't had credit before or because of your past sins, start building a strong track record. This takes years. There are no quick fixes.

- Pay *all* your bills, *on time,* all the time.
- *(Re)build some credit*. One way is to get a credit card in your name. If you can't get a regular credit card, get a *secured card* which requires you to deposit some cash up-front. Spend only a little every month. For example, set up automatic payment of your cellphone bill using the credit card and then set up automatic payment of the credit card bill from your checking account on payday. Keep the card tucked away in a drawer and leave it there.
- Do not use more than about 25% of any credit line to keep your *credit utilization* low.
- *Freeze your credit* file at each of the three bureaus.

Freeze Your Credit

Your credit file is an open book. Many types of lenders can request it without your permission in order to "market" to you. It's how credit bureaus make money—they sell your info.

While you can "opt out" of pre-screened offers, the best way to combat this is to freeze your credit file at each of the three bureaus. This prevents *all* "pulls" of your credit file. (It does not stop your credit information from being updated.) By law, the bureaus must offer this capability for free. They used to make it cumbersome to do. It's easier since Equifax experienced a major privacy breach in 2017. But beware of attempts to push other paid "services" such as "credit locks" or "credit monitoring." Insist on a freeze.

A freeze has three benefits: it protects your privacy and identity by preventing anyone from pulling your credit file without your permission, it reduces unwanted credit solicitations, and it is a barrier against the temptation of instant credit offers.

Before you apply for a major loan such as a mortgage or private student loan review your credit reports to make sure there are no errors on them. Then unfreeze your credit files for two weeks while you shop around for a loan. Avoid triggering a lot of credit inquiries from banks over a longer period as this could be bad for your score.

Credit Builder "Loans"

The wider use of credit scores has created new ways for financial companies to reach into your pocket, particularly if you're already vulnerable. Enter the "credit builder loan." Here's how it works. This one is from **Self Financial**, an on-line company with a millennial feel and a snazzy website: Pay us $35 a month for two years, plus a $9 fee, for a total of $849. In two years, we'll give you $724 of your money back. We keep the rest (info as of 1/4/2021).

Why would anyone take such a terrible deal? The pitch is that if you demonstrate an ability to make regular payments it might improve your credit score. Research suggests that more often than not this doesn't happen.[24] Think about it. Credit builder loans are "loans" where you don't actually get money up-front. There is no risk to the lender that you won't "pay back" the loan. Still, Self charges 15.97% APR on this "loan" (that's the $125 difference between the money you pay and what you get back.) You can find more reasonable rates at other "lenders," but that doesn't make them a good deal. With these schemes not only are you *charged* "interest," but you also give up the opportunity to shop around and *earn* the best interest on the money you pay.

To improve your credit score, it is better to make your periodic payments into a savings account. Once you've accumulated a balance of about $200, use those savings to get a secured credit card.

[24] Consumer Financial Protection Bureau, "Targeting Credit Builder Loans," July 2020.

Resources

Government or Regulatory Agencies and Mandates		
NMLS Resource Center	Check whether your mortgage broker or lender is licensed	**https://www.nmlsconsumeraccess.org/**
Department of Education	Find out more about federal student loans	**https://studentaid.ed.gov/sa/**
Central Source LLC (sponsored by Equifax, Experian and Transunion)	Get your free annual credit reports. The only site providing federally mandated free reports	**www.annualcreditreport.com**
Consumer Financial Protection Bureau (CFPB)	Obtain information on credit counseling	**https://www.consumerfinance.gov/**

Businesses		
Fair Isaac Corporation	Learn how FICO scores work	**www.myfico.com**
Bankrate.com	Compare interest rates and loan offerings. Paid by the companies they display. Also have a **calculator** to estimate payments for a consolidation loan.	**https://www.bankrate.com/**
Credit Karma	Obtain Transunion and Equifax credit scores and reports for free. They gather lots of data on you in return. Paid by companies they display	**https://www.creditkarma.com/**
National Foundation for Credit Counseling (NFCC), a trade group supported by financial companies	Obtain information on debt management programs and referrals to debt counselors	**https://www.nfcc.org/**
Financial Counseling Association of America (FCAA), a member-supported trade group of financial counselors	Obtain information on debt management programs and referrals to debt counselors	**https://fcaa.org/**
Upsolve	A non-profit that provides an app for completing paperwork for bankruptcy without paying attorneys' fees	**https://upsolve.org/**

Chapter 10: Money for Later

Mr. Simms (bank interviewer): "Do you have any experience?"

Robbie Hart: "No, sir, I have no experience but I'm a big fan of money. I like it, I use it, I have a little. I keep it in a jar on top of my refrigerator. I'd like to put more in that jar. That's where you come in."

– The Wedding Singer (1998)

Borrowing pulls money from the future for spending today. You *pay* interest for the privilege, reducing your lifetime money pile and making bankers a little richer. Saving does the opposite. You put money in the jar, pushing it from today into the future. You *earn* interest and grow your pile.

The concept of saving is simple. The problem is finding the money to put aside. For this you need some income, and you need discipline. Then you need to figure out the best jar to put the money in, which involves taking advantage of tax breaks the government put in place to encourage saving.

How to Save

To some people, saving comes easy. They cherish frugality. They don't mind living well below their means, with fewer things, in smaller houses, driving older cars. If you're one of those people, you can skip this section.

For others, saving seems impossible. There is never money left after paying the bills. Every month brings a new unexpected expense. Your account balances always hover around zero. If this is you, here are a few tips for getting started and ramping up your savings.

Start Small, but Start

Most everyone can afford to save. Saving 20% as suggested by the 50-30-20 rule may seem crazy out of reach today. Don't worry about it. Save a small amount even if you're paying off a pile of debt. To quote track star Jim Ryun, "Motivation is what gets you started, habit is what keeps you going." This step is about building habits.

Start with amounts that you won't notice. If you pay for things with cash, throw any change in a bowl every night. If you use a debit card, check out cards that "round up" your purchases to the nearest dollar and put the change into a savings account. The original "round-up" card was from **Acorns**, but others have sprouted, including on-line bank **Chime** and **Keep the Change** from Bank of America.

You shouldn't have to pay any fees for these services, which are only going to become more commonplace. And these apps pay stingy interest, so plan on moving the money to your high-yield savings account once you accumulate more than $100. Acorns is a little different, because instead of a savings account you get a brokerage account. More on those in Chapter 13.[25]

Next, set up an automatic transfer from your checking account to your savings account every payday. Even if it's just $5. In six months, increase it to $10. Better yet, see if your employer can split your paycheck and send a specified amount directly to your savings account.

---

[25] Acorns charges a reasonable $3 per month fee for a three-account combination: checking account, investment account, and IRA account, and provides other benefits such as free ATM withdrawals.

Save at Work

Your most important savings are for retirement. You might say, "Oh, that's far away." As we'll see in later chapters, that's exactly why you should do it today. Time is huge when it comes to retirement saving. So take advantage of retirement savings plans at work.

If your employer offers a 401(k) or 403(b) plan start by making sure to get the full amount of any company match. Not all employers offer a match and there are many different formulas. A common one is for the employer to contribute half of the amount each worker contributes, up to a maximum of 3%.[26] If a worker saves 3% of their pay, the employer will add another 1.5%. If the worker contributes 6%, the employer will add the maximum of 3%.

Raise the Bar

With a modest saving program up and running, it's time to step things up. Try to push savings to 5% or 10% of money coming in. However, don't do this if you are still paying off high-cost debt. Pay down debt first. As you reduce debt, the freed-up money that previously went to paying interest is available for savings. Build up an emergency fund first, then work on increasing your retirement and other savings.

Another way to raise the bar is to dedicate pay increases to savings. Say you get a 2% annual raise. Immediately increase your savings by the same amount and continue to live on the budget you were used to. If you can't do the full 2%, split the difference and save 1%.

Harvest Windfalls

Sometimes good things happen, and we have financial windfalls: bonuses, gifts, tax refunds, raffle or other winnings, and inheritances. Use these windfalls to boost savings instead of spending. Take all or

---

[26] Dayana Yochim, "Does Your Company's 401(k) Plan Stack Up With Everyone Else's?," Marketwatch.com, 6/14/2019.

part of them and immediately transfer them to your savings account. You won't miss spending them.

Where to Save

The question of where to put the money that you save mostly hinges on taxes. The government provides significant help when you save for three things: retirement, education, and health care. There are some smaller incentives, but those are the biggies.

Saving for Retirement

Let's start with retirement. We have already covered some of this in Chapter 3, but here is a more general overview.

Your retirement savings should be in a retirement account. If you have a defined contribution plan such as a 401(k) or 403(b) plan at work, contribute to it. Otherwise use an *Individual Retirement Account (IRA)*. These are so-called *qualified* retirement accounts. Qualified accounts have more restrictions but also more tax benefits and better protections than *non-qualified* accounts.

The basic idea behind retirement accounts is this: you owe taxes on money you earn from work, but when you put that money into a retirement account the *investment income* is not taxed. Your money grows tax-free. There are two basic ways to accomplish this: pay taxes before you contribute to an account or pay taxes when you take the money out.

Contributions to Account	Investment Income	Withdrawals from Account	Types of accounts
Not taxed (contribute "pre-tax" dollars)	Not taxed	Taxed	"Traditional"" 401 (k) plans "Traditional" IRAs
Taxed (contribute "after-tax" dollars)	Not taxed	Not taxed	"Roth" 401 (k) plans "Roth" IRAs

The two are mathematically equivalent *if* your tax rate is the same when you withdraw as it is when you contribute. This is why one of the early choices you may face in your career is whether to save in a "traditional" or a "Roth" account. How do you know which is better? If your tax rate is lower in retirement, a traditional account will end up being the better choice. If it's higher, a Roth account will be better. Of course, you don't know what it will be in advance. So you have to make some assumptions.

When you are early in your career and your salary (and tax rate) are low, a Roth account is probably a good bet. If you're a high earner, your tax rate may be lower in retirement, so go with a traditional account. To be safe, you may want to contribute to some of each. But don't get hung up on this decision. The most important thing is to start contributing as much as you can as early as possible.

The government provides a good deal on retirement accounts, so you probably won't be surprised that the deal comes with some strings attached. Here are the major ones:

- There are limits to how much you can contribute. These usually change every year. For example, in 2021 the most you can contribute to a 401(k) or 403(b) account and get the tax break is $19,500. For an IRA the limit is $6,000. If you're self-employed there are other options with higher limits.
- There are also restrictions on taking money out early. One is the magic age of 59½ (don't ask). You can face penalties for taking out money before then unless it is for certain specified purposes.
- With traditional (but not Roth) accounts you *have to* start taking some money out when you turn 72 even if you don't need it. That's okay, you'll just put in regular savings. But you will owe tax on those "required minimum distributions" or RMDs.

There are lots of other intricacies and options with retirement accounts to dig into if you find that you have extra money to save. I hope you have that problem.

Saving for Education

The best way to save for college is with a so-called *529 plan* (another snazzy name brought to you courtesy of the IRS). Also known as *qualified tuition plans*, 529 plans are sponsored by states, so they come in a wide variety of flavors, some better than others. They all have federal tax benefits very similar to a Roth retirement account: you put in after-tax dollars, your savings grow tax free, and you owe no tax when you withdraw the money…as long as you use it to pay for education expenses.

A 529 plan account has an *owner* who controls the account and a *beneficiary* who will receive the money to attend a school or university. The two can be the same person. The owner can change the beneficiary to another family member at any time without losing any tax benefits. This means you can start saving for a child's education even before it is born by making yourself the beneficiary.

Another type of account is the *Coverdell Education Savings Account (ESA)*. Up to $2,000 a year can be put into an ESA. The tax benefit is similar to a 529 plan. But you shouldn't add money after the beneficiary is eighteen years old. The main benefit of ESAs is that they can be used for a somewhat wider range of education expenses.

Don't think of these accounts as just for a child's college. Both can also be used for primary and secondary schools, as well as graduate school.

The third way to save for education is through *U.S. Savings Bonds*. These are bought directly from the Treasury Department. They pay a small interest rate but are guaranteed by the U.S. government and won't lose money. You don't owe tax on any interest when you cash them in as long as the money is used for educational expenses or is put into a 529 plan for later use. But you must be at least twenty-four years old when you buy the bonds and your income cannot exceed certain limits in the year you redeem them.

The ability to save for education without paying taxes is very valuable. When it comes to taking out the money things get tricky as to how much and which education expenses qualify, so be sure to get additional guidance.

Choosing a 529 Plan

There is a cottage industry devoted to helping you find the "best" 529 Plan. Much of this "help" is from salespeople trying to make money. In making your choice, be sure to focus on three things: 1) Having good, low-cost investment selections. Having good options is more important than having a lot of options (see Chapter 14); 2) Taking advantage of any state income tax breaks, usually by choosing a plan sponsored by your state; 3) Choosing a plan with low or no administrative fees. Ideally you should be able to set up automatic contributions and not think about your 529 Plan again until it's time to withdraw money. The National Association of State Treasurers provides a **tool** for comparing different state plans.

Saving for Healthcare

It is particularly hard to save for healthcare because medical expenses are unpredictable. If at all possible, you should get insurance to cover the potentially devastating costs of a major illness or accident. But insurance is expensive and it may or may not cover more routine expenses such as needed prescriptions, dentist visits, vision expenses, health screenings and checkups, counseling, or physical therapy, to name just a few.

You can sign up or change your health insurance once a year, usually in November or December. If you are healthy and aren't planning on any major expenses—such as an elective surgery or childbirth—you might consider one of the best saving deals available: a *healthcare savings account (HSA).* With an HSA you don't pay taxes when you contribute or when you withdraw money. It's completely tax-free as long as the money is used to pay for healthcare expenses.

Unfortunately, not everyone can contribute to an HSA. To do so you must enroll in a *high deductible health plan (HDHP)*. Again, if you have high medical expenses this may not be the best option. And if your employer or insurance company doesn't offer one, you're out of luck. But if they do, I recommend taking full advantage of it, even before saving in a 401(k) beyond the employer match, especially if your employer also makes a contribution to the HSA. You can let the money in an HSA grow tax-free for years and use it to pay healthcare expenses, including Medicare premiums, when you're old.[27]

Many HSA accounts have limited (and lousy) investment options and charge too many fees. However, *Fidelity* began offering them with no minimums or fees and investment options comparable to a brokerage account. This makes them the go-to for HSAs.[28] If your employer enrolls you in a lousy HSA by default you can transfer or "roll over" your balance to Fidelity once a year.

There is another savings deal offered by many employers: a so-called *flexible spending account (FSA)***.** These also allow you to put in pre-tax money and use it to pay for medical expenses. They are tricky, though, because you have to spend all the money in the year in which you contribute it. That means you need to guess beforehand how much in medical expenses you'll have in the coming year. Anything you don't spend, you lose. Still, if managed well FSAs are a good deal.[29]

---

[27] One technique is to use other money to pay for routine health-related costs and save receipts. Let your HSA savings grow tax-free. When you take money out later you can use it for *anything* as long as you can show that you spent that amount on healthcare while the account was open.

[28] Leo Acheson and Megan Pacholok, "Our 2019 Rankings of 11 Top HSA Providers," Morningstar.com, 10/1/2019.

[29] Some employers also offer separate flexible spending accounts that can be used for childcare or dependent care expenses.

Saving for Everything Else

We've covered the main tax-advantaged ways to save. They all come with restrictions on when you can get at the money or what it can be used for. What about other savings goals?

A common one is to save up for a *down payment on a home*. While the government doesn't have a tax break for this, you are allowed to withdraw funds from an IRA to buy a first home, and you're also allowed to take a long-term loan from your 401(k). (The IRS considers any home your "first" if you haven't owned one in the prior two years.) It's a bit risky though, because you potentially put a big dent in your retirement kitty. Proceed with care!

What about saving for fun stuff? Sorry, but Uncle Sam won't pitch in for your jet ski or Disney cruise with a tax break. That doesn't mean you shouldn't save—in fact, you should save rather than borrow for this kind of thing. Let's call this "regular" savings.

In terms of the best places to put regular savings, we've already covered *high-yield savings accounts* and *certificates of deposit*. These are low risk options that don't earn much interest. Stick with them for money that you want to access in the next five years.

For goals more than five years out you may want to shoot for a higher return and open a *brokerage account*. Brokerage accounts let you buy a wide variety of investments like stocks and bonds. If you're at this point, we're ready to take a walk down Wall Street. Hold on to your hat!

Resources

Government and Regulatory Agencies		
Securities and Exchange Commission	Information on 529 plans	**https://www.sec.gov/**
FINRA	Information on saving for college	**https://www.finra.org/investors/**
College Savings Plan Network	Site affiliated with the National Association of State Treasurers (provides resources and tools on 529 plans)	**https://www.collegesavings.org/**
TreasuryDirect	Buy savings bonds directly from the government.	**https://treasurydirect.gov/**
IRS	Publication 969 on HSA Accounts	**https://www.irs.gov/**

Businesses		
Savingforcollege.com	Information on 529 plans, student loans and related topics. Paid for by advertising and referrals	**https://www.savingforcollege.com/**
Devenir	Provides a tool to compare HSA providers	**https://info.hsasearch.com/**

Chapter 11: Money on The Street

Dominick Amato: "I hear all you guys on Wall Street are millionaires. When you gonna make us rich?"

Bud Fox: "Gotta open an account to win the lottery, Dominick. Give me $15,000, you'll have a condo in Florida next Christmas."

– Wall Street (1987)

If you're ready to save for longer-term goals you should get a brokerage account. This will get you admission to "Wall Street", the global world of finance and investing that draws its name from a few short city blocks in downtown New York. Both are worth a visit.

A brokerage account lets you buy and sell different types of investments, which you cannot do in a checking or savings account. A regular brokerage account is "taxable," just like a regular bank account. This means that if you earn interest or other kinds of investment income in the account you will owe taxes on that income. But you can also have IRA or Roth IRA brokerage accounts, with the tax benefits mentioned in the last chapter.

Choosing where to open a brokerage account can be overwhelming—and overwhelmingly dull. In the interest of your sanity, I'm going to narrow the choice to just a handful.

There is a rough distinction between "full-service" and "discount" brokerage firms. Full-service brokerages often end up being costly because they have "financial advisors" who are paid to sell you investments. Among the biggest are *Edward Jones*, *Raymond James*, *Merrill Lynch* (owned by *Bank of America*), *Wells Fargo Advisors*, *Ameriprise*, and *Morgan Stanley*. I suggest staying away from them to keep expenses to a minimum.

Discount brokerages are more or less self-service. They have comprehensive, easy-to-use websites that allow you to research, buy, and sell investments. If you get stuck, they have phone support. Some also have branch offices that you can visit for various services. The biggest are **Fidelity**, **Schwab**, and **E*Trade**. All of them handle traditional and Roth IRAs. Fidelity also offers HSA accounts. For the investment approach that I espouse in this book, I suggest you sign up with either Fidelity, Schwab, or **Vanguard**. Vanguard has some of the best low-cost mutual funds, which may not be available for free at Schwab or Fidelity. Vanguard's website is a bit clunkier, but it works.

There are a host of other brokerage account options. Most likely you don't need them. Here's why:

- If you want to work with a financial advisor, you may be asked to go with the company he or she is affiliated with. This could be a bank, insurance company, or so-called advisor platform (such as *LPL Financial*). But having your brokerage account through one of these entities can be more expensive and less flexible. If you want an advisor, consider one who doesn't require you to keep your money with them. At a minimum, be very aware of any extra fees you are being charged—directly or through the investment choices offered (see Chapter 25).
- On-line start-up *Robinhood* has a millennial vibe but a limited offering. When they first hit the scene they forced other big discount brokers to eliminate commissions, but at this point their services don't keep up with Fidelity or Schwab. Also, Robinhood tries to entice you to manage your portfolio on your phone. As we'll discuss in a later chapter, constantly checking up on your portfolio is a recipe for making bad choices.

- You may come across so-called *robo-advisors*, among the most prominent of which are *Wealthfront* and *Betterment*. While these are brokerage accounts in name, they don't give you the freedom to choose your investments. Instead, for a fee, they serve up investments predetermined by an algorithm. Similar services are cropping up at most major brokerage firms. If you nevertheless want a robo, Schwab offers a no-fee version through its *Intelligent Portfolios*.
- Some mutual fund companies—for example *T. Rowe Price*—offer brokerage accounts. These are largely an afterthought. Mutual fund companies are in business to sell you *their* funds.
- There are firms that cater specifically to active traders. *Interactive Brokers* is one of the largest.

Once you have opened a brokerage account, have a portion of your paycheck deposited into it and start saving. You should also link it to your checking account so you can make additional deposits. Your money will initially be parked in the brokerage firm's *sweep account* until you use it to invest in something. A sweep account is simply a very safe investment option (often a *money market fund*) that is set up not to lose money but also does not pay a lot of interest.

How safe is your money in a brokerage account? Unlike bank accounts, the *value* of brokerage accounts is not guaranteed by the government or anyone else. If you invest in something that loses money, it's on you. But pretty much every brokerage firm is a member of the Securities Industry Protection Corporation (SIPC). The SIPC is not a government agency. It gets its money from its members. Using this money, the SIPC steps in if the firm at which you have your accounts goes bust or defrauds you. It will pay up to $500,000 per person. Don't get an account at a firm that doesn't display "Member SIPC."[30]

---

[30] See www.sipc.org/for-investors/what-sipc-protects and www.finra.org/investors/have-problem/your-rights-under-sipc-protection for more on SIPC protection.

Chapter 12: Money from Money

Obanno: "Do you believe in God, Mr. Le Chiffre?"

Le Chiffre: "No. I believe in a reasonable rate of return"

– Casino Royale (2006)

This chapter is about making money without working. (Applause!) How? By buying things that you expect will make a profit—in other words, by *investing*. Almost anything you buy with a plan to sell it for more than you paid can be an investment. In this book we will focus on the main types of financial investments, stocks and bonds.

The profit you make from an investment is its *return*. Often there are two parts of return: one is *yield*, which are regular payments such as *interest* from a bond or *dividends* from a stock; the second is *capital gains*, which are the profits from selling something for a higher price than you bought it for. Capital gains are *unrealized* if the value has increased but you have not yet sold. They can shrink or even become *capital losses* if the price of the thing goes down. Capital gains are *realized* once you've sold. Add up yield and capital gains and you get *total return*.

The total return of an investment is reduced by *investment expenses*. Investment expenses are, pick your adjective, pernicious, insidious, sneaky. They seem harmless. They are often expressed as a small percentage of the amount in your account. It's not uncommon to see expenses of 1% of your account balance each year. And you might say, "Oh, 1% isn't a whole lot." But look at this example:

What Would $5,000 Invested in Stocks in 1990 Be Worth After 30 Years?

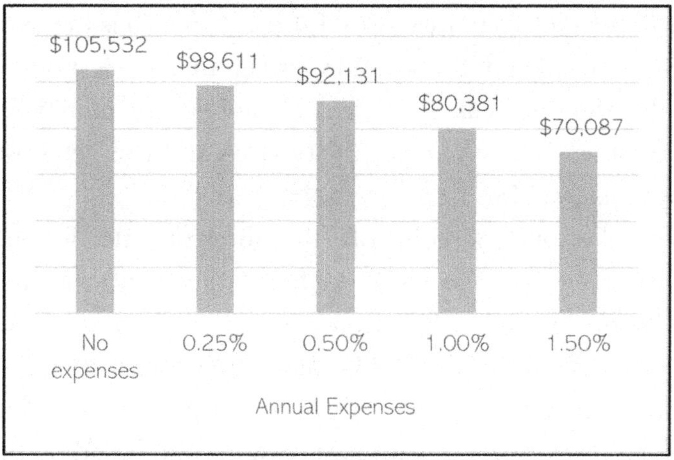

If you had been able to invest $5,000 in the S&P 500 stock index at the end of 1990, the total return of the index without paying any expenses over the next thirty years would have increased the value to $105,532 by the end of 2020.

If you had paid someone 1% of your account every year to "manage" your investment you'd only have $80,381. Ugh!

Investment expenses are one of the few things about investing you actually control. These days there are many options to keep them below 0.25%, or even below 0.1%.

There is very little that any investment manager or advisor does to justify skimming a quarter of your retirement money off the top.

Compounding Explained

What is going on in this example? Why does 1% make such a difference over a long time? The reason is that investment returns *compound.* Compounding means that the investment income you earn in one period earns returns in all the following periods.

Bear with me for just a little math...

If I deposit \$100 in account and earn 10% annual interest[31], in a year I will have \$110 (\$100 x 1.1). If I stay invested another year, that \$110 will turn into \$121 (\$100 x 1.1 x 1.1, which is the same as \$100 x 1.1^2). Notice that in the second year I earned interest on the interest I earned in the first year. Each period I *multiply* my money by one plus the interest rate. Do this over thirty years and you get \$100 x 1.1^{30}, which equals \$1,745.

Now take one percent off the interest rate for investment expenses. After one year I have \$109 (\$100 x 1.09). Just a dollar less than with no expenses. But after thirty years I have \$100 x 1.09^{30}, which equals \$1,327. That's *24% less* money than with no expenses.

Some financial products only offer *simple interest.* With simple interest you earn the same amount each period, based on the original deposit. Simple interest is not multiplied, it's just added. The first year of simple interest is the same as with compound interest: \$100 + \$10 = \$110. In year two you start to fall behind: \$100 + \$10 + \$10 = \$120. Not much of a difference at first. But look at what happens over thirty years: \$100 + \$10 + \$10 + \$10...etc. = \$400. By the time you reach thirty years, 10% simple interest is the equivalent of just 0.3% compound interest. Here is a picture:

[31] I am using "interest" here, but the math works for any constant return, whether yield, capital gains, or a combination of both.

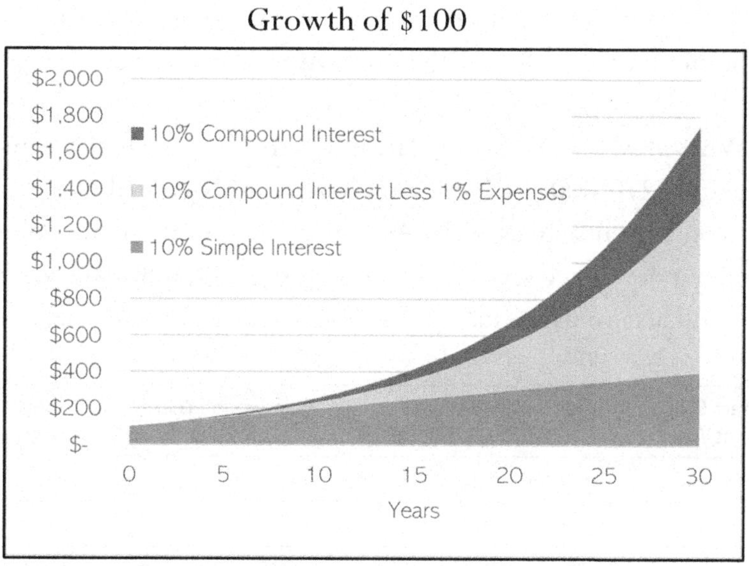

What are the takeaways?

- The power of compounding comes over time. Notice it's not until after about five years that the lines diverge.
- A small difference in return costs you big.
- Simple interest sucks.

Sometimes it's helpful to turn the calculation around. Go back to the earlier illustration of investing $5,000 in the S&P 500 stock index in 1990. That initial dollar amount grew by some compound return to reach $105,532. We need to find the rate, *r*, that solves the equation $\$5{,}000 \times (1 + r)^{30} = \$105{,}532$. A little algebra and a calculator will tell you that $r = 10.7\%$. This is the annual compound return of the S&P 500 over the thirty years ending in 2020.

You Can Start Early Only Once

Let's return to the simple example from Chapter 2. Recall we earned annual income of $60,000 over forty-five working years, or a total of $2,700,000. What if *right away* we start saving $500 a month for retirement? We'll sock away $270,000 in total (a 10% savings rate). Now if we earn an average of 5% a year by investing, we accumulate $1,017,441 by the time we are ready to retire at age sixty-five.[32]

What if we start saving later? Even if we save the same total amount, $270,000, by increasing our monthly contribution to $643, we won't do nearly as well. As you can see in the table below, our "money pile" at age sixty-five is now just $733,388. And so on: start later and accumulate much less *even when saving the exact same amount*.

Start Saving at Age	Monthly Saving for $270,000 Total	Number of Years to Save	Money Pile at Age 65
20	$500	45	$1,017,441
30	$643	35	$733,388
40	$900	25	$538,192
50	$1,500	15	$402,604

I hope this convinces you of the power of compounding, and the importance of starting to save early. And of course, we each get only one chance to start early. When she's gone, she's gone.

[32] This is the future value of an annuity due. You can calculate your own at www.calculator.net/future-value-calculator.html.

Chapter 13: The Smart Money

Gary Burns (TV interviewer): "So you're saying, Mr. Gardiner, if the stock market collapses, and unemployment keeps increasing, that this is just another season, so to speak, in the garden?"

Chance the Gardener: "Yes. In a garden, things grow – but first some things must wither; some trees lose their leaves before they grow new leaves... And if you give your garden a lot of love, and if you work very hard and have a lot of patience, in the proper season you will see it grow to be very beautiful..."

– Being There (1979)

Here is something you might hear: Investing is like driving a car. You don't need to know engines and transmissions. You rely on the engineers and mechanics to make sure your car works as it should. Likewise, don't worry about what goes on inside your investments. They were designed by experts. Trust the financial engineers to have gotten it right.

I really don't like this argument. It's patronizing. It's a bad analogy because financial engineering is not like mechanical or electrical engineering. And most people actually do know the major components of a car. They certainly learn where the gas pedal and the brakes are.

So, to keep from skidding off the road, anyone who invests should know the following basic types of *securities* that are bought and sold in the financial markets.

Stocks

If you own a *stock*, you own a piece of a company. Stocks come in *shares*, because each one entitles you to a share of the company's profits and a vote when the company elects its board of directors. In Chapter 5 we saw how an individual's net worth represents the difference between the assets and liabilities on their balance sheet. It's the same with companies. A share of stock is a share of a company's net worth—its assets minus its liabilities. Another word for net worth is *equity*, so stocks are often referred to as *equities*.

Companies are *public* if they have *listed* their shares on a stock exchange so that anyone can buy or sell them. The price at which shares are traded changes all the time depending on supply and demand. Companies on the stock exchanges are often identified by their *ticker symbols*. For example, Apple's symbol is AAPL, Facebook's FB, Netflix's NFLX.

Although some stock exchanges are physical locations such as the New York Stock Exchange, these days most buying and selling happens electronically. You and I can trade public stocks on most exchanges from our computer if we have a brokerage account.

To track how the overall stock market is doing, people came up with *stock indices*. The granddaddy of indices is the *Dow Jones Industrial Average*, which is a group of thirty large companies that are representative of the American economy. The index tracks the change in the average of these companies' stock prices.[33] The other two indices to be aware of are the *Standard and Poor's 500 (S&P 500)* index, which is composed of about 500 of the largest companies, and the

---

[33] The list of companies included changes from time to time as some become less relevant or go out of business and others grow in importance.

Nasdaq Composite index. This index consists of all the stocks listed on the Nasdaq, an electronic stock exchange favored by many tech companies.

Many companies pay *dividends* to their shareholders. The idea is that dividends are a way to pay some of the company's profits to shareholders in cash, but it is completely up to the company whether and how much to pay. There is no obligation to pay dividends, and a lot of companies don't. Especially growing companies often choose to put their profits back into the business rather than pay dividends.

Over the long term, stock prices have gone up, though there have been big declines, some of which lasted for years. What makes the stock market go up? The best explanation is that the value of companies increases with economic growth. This does not help with predicting what the market will do tomorrow, next week, or even next year. In fact, over the short term, the chances of the market going up or down are close to even (like flipping a coin). Sure, if you look at the news there are always many "explanations" for market movements. But they always explain the past, never the future.

Bonds

Bonds are a different animal from stocks. As we saw, when you buy a stock you buy a little piece of a company. You don't know whether you'll receive dividends and whether the company will be a successful business that increases in value. When you buy a bond you are making a loan. The bond is an I.O.U. that promises specific interest payments and the *principal* back at the end. This is known as the *maturity* date.

The biggest borrower (called an *issuer* of bonds) is the U.S. Government. It regularly issues *Treasury securities* to pay for government spending. These "Treasurys" are bonds that can have maturities between one month and thirty years.[34]

Companies also issue bonds, as do state and municipal governments and other entities. Most people consider Treasurys to be the safest bonds because the risk that the U.S. government won't pay back its debt is very small.

When people talk about interest rates going up or down, they are often talking about the interest rate on Treasurys. Directly or indirectly, most other interest rates are influenced by Treasury interest rates. That's true for both interest you *earn*, for example on corporate bonds and savings accounts, and for interest you *pay* on mortgages, student loans, and other debt.

Just as with stocks, people calculate indices to track different groups of bonds. But the more common way to look at the bond market is the Treasury *yield curve*, which is simply a snapshot of Treasury interest rates with different maturities. Here is what the yield curve looked like on March 15, 2021:

Treasury Yield Curve (March 15, 2021)

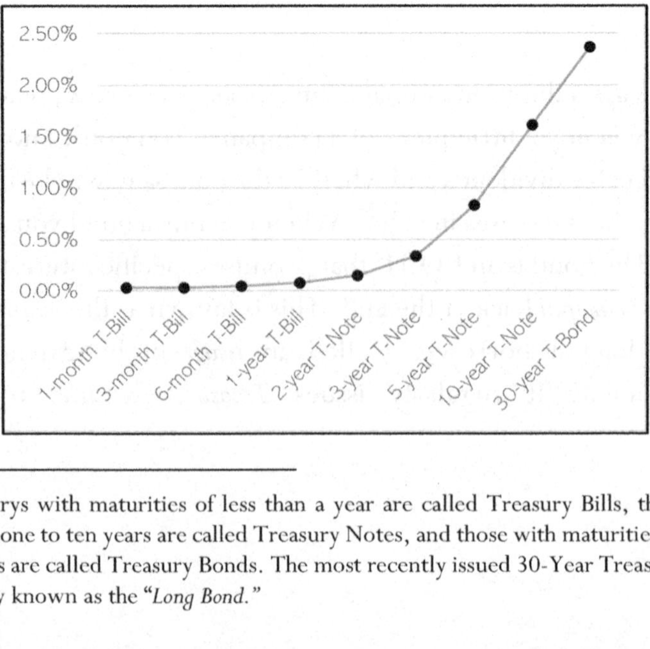

[34] Treasurys with maturities of less than a year are called Treasury Bills, those with maturities of one to ten years are called Treasury Notes, and those with maturities of more than ten years are called Treasury Bonds. The most recently issued 30-Year Treasury Bond is colloquially known as the "*Long Bond.*"

Interest rates change every day and the prices of bonds fluctuate accordingly. When interest rates go up, bond prices go down, and when interest rates go down, bond prices go up.[35]

Remember certificates of deposit (CDs)? We went over them when talking about savings accounts in Chapter 4. CDs are also a little like bonds: they pay you a pre-determined amount of interest for a pre-determined period of time. But they are insured by the federal government (the FDIC) and therefore are guaranteed to pay back the principal. This makes them a good alternative to bonds when you want to have your savings available at a particular time in the future.

Inflation-Protected Bonds

In Chapter 1 we talked about the role of money as a store of value, and how inflation reduces the value of money over time. One of the main reasons for investing is to make sure that savings don't get eaten away by inflation.

Historically, investing in the stock market has beaten inflation by a lot. But that's not true over every period, nor is it guaranteed in to be the case in the future. If you want to be sure that your savings keep up with inflation there are two types of bonds that do just that. Both are issued by the government.

---

[35] This can be a source of confusion. To get the intuition try the following example. Say you just bought a bond for $100 that will pay you back $100 when it matures and interest of 3% ($3 a year) in the meantime. The next day interest rates in the market go to 4%. If you try to sell your bond now, buyers won't give you $100 for your 3% bond because newly issued bonds earn 4% ($4 a year). They'll pay you a price that makes the $3 a year equivalent to a 4% interest rate. What's that price? That depends on the maturity of the bond: if it is close to maturity (perhaps an interest payment or two to go) it may be $98 to make up for a couple of payments of $3 instead of $4. If the bond has ten years to go, the discount is going to be much larger; perhaps it'll only be worth $90. Note that while the market value of the bond goes down today, it still pays back principal of $100 back when it matures. The fact that you lose out on some interest in the meantime is what makes it worth less.

The first is a special Treasury called *Treasury Inflation Protected Securities* or *TIPS*. Just like regular Treasurys, TIPS come with different maturities. But with TIPS, the principal of the bond increases with inflation. They start out with the same principal as every other new Treasury, $1,000 per bond. But unlike regular Treasurys, which pay back the same principal of $1,000 at maturity, the principal of TIPS increases by the amount of inflation. If inflation in the second year is 2%, the principal increases to $1,020. The interest rate on TIPS is low, even zero sometimes, but your money is guaranteed to keep pace with inflation.

The second is a type of savings bond. (We met savings bonds when talking about saving for education expenses.) *Series I Savings Bonds*, or *I-Bonds* for short, keep up with inflation by paying an interest rate that is equal to the rate of inflation plus some small, fixed amount. I-Bonds can't be bought in a brokerage account. You need to buy them directly from the Treasury Department. You can easily open an account to do this at **TreasuryDirect**.

Mutual Funds and ETFs

We're going to switch gears now to two types of investments that should be the workhorses of your portfolio: *mutual funds* and *exchange traded funds (ETFs)*.[36] In both cases you are buying shares in a *fund* that in turn owns many other stocks, bonds, and other sometimes other financial instruments. You end up owning not one stock or bond, but tiny slices of hundreds or thousands of stocks or bonds with a single purchase.

Funds are managed by investment companies who charge fees to put them together and make sure they stick to their investment objectives. Those fees are reflected in the funds' *expense ratios*, which

[36] The differences between mutual funds and ETFs are not terribly important. The main one is that the price of mutual funds is only updated once a day, whereas ETFs continuously trade on the stock exchange. What does matter is what they are invested in.

are expressed as a percentage of the assets in the fund. When you buy a fund, its expense ratio is the percentage of your money that goes to pay for managing the fund each year. Recall the importance of keeping expense ratios to a minimum from the discussion on compounding.

There are thousands of mutual funds and ETFs to choose from. You can ignore most of them. In the next chapter I will give you a short list of low-cost *index funds*, so called because they hold the stocks (or bonds) that make up a particular index. They don't try to pick winners or losers; they just try to match the performance of the index. They are all you need to get started investing.

Everything Else

There is a vast universe of specialized mutual funds, ETFs, and other investments that I haven't covered. These are the bread and butter—or rather the Ferraris and yachts—of the investment business. As the jargon gets fancier and the sales pitch slicker, the costs go up.

Here are some investing strategies (and buzzwords) that you might encounter but aren't worth paying extra for:

- Dividend or "income" strategies
- Small-cap, mid-cap, large-cap, value, or growth strategies
- "Smart beta" such as "momentum," "quality," and other "long-short" strategies
- Managed futures, tactical allocation, managed volatility, market neutral, risk parity strategies

What else? In uncertain times people sometimes want to own *gold*. There is a sense of security about it. You feel rich just holding it. But planning to sell it at a profit during retirement to buy groceries is risky. Gold and other *commodities* have very volatile prices and, contrary to what you might hear, haven't done a good job protecting against inflation.

Bitcoin? We talked about bitcoin as a currency in Chapter1. As an investment it's highly speculative and largely unproven over longer periods of time. You will hear stories from crypto evangelists who say bitcoin is the future. You'll hear others scoff and dismiss it out of hand. It has had more staying power than the pessimists expected, but nobody really knows what the future of crypto will be. Your call.

Real estate? Not for most people, for three reasons. One, if you own your home, you are already investing in real estate with each mortgage payment. Two, people who make a lot of money in real estate are those who are in that business: developers, landlords, fund managers. These are jobs, not investments. Three, you already get a healthy slug of real estate investments as part of your stock index funds.

The day may come when you're eligible for membership in a special club: you can be an *accredited investor.* [37] Now your broker's eyes will really light up because he can sell you "alternative" investments: private real estate funds, hedge funds, venture capital, or private equity, among other things. The pitch: You too can be part of the "smart money"! The truth: Unless you are already worth many millions or have special connections you will *not* get ground-floor access to the next Amazon or Facebook. But you *will* pay large hidden costs, give up access to your money when you want it, and be kept in the dark about exactly what it is invested in.

---

[37] Accredited investors are required to have annual income of $200,000 or a net worth of $1,000,000 (excluding their primary residence).

Brokerage Account Statements

Brokerage account statements are tedious and confusing. They have separate categories for stocks, fixed income (bonds), ETFs, and mutual funds, as though these were somehow comparable categories. They're not. With funds you need to know what's *inside* them to understand what you own. If the funds you own in turn invest in stocks, they should be added to your stock total; if they own bonds, they should be added to your bond total, if they own a combination, they need to be split between categories.

Fortunately, the websites of the brokerage firms have analyses that "look through" to the underlying investments in any funds. Use these tools instead of account statements to understand what's in your portfolio.

Chapter 14: Risk and Money

Lloyd: "Come on, give it to me straight. I drove a long way to see you. The least you can do is level with me. What are my chances?"

Mary: "Not good."

Lloyd: "You mean not good, like one out of a hundred?"

Mary: "I'd say more like one out of a million."

Lloyd: "So you're telling me there's a chance... YEAH!"

– Dumb and Dumber (1994)

Investing in stocks and bonds is your best bet for getting a better return than putting all your money in a savings account. But there's a hitch. You could end up losing money instead. This is called "risk." *You cannot expect to earn higher returns without taking more risk.*

How do you measure risk? Finance geeks calculate how much returns bounce around from period to period. They measure *volatility.*[38] For example, take the last day of each month since 1946. Look at the total return you would have had if your money had been invested in the S&P 500 stock index over the previous year, ending on that day. In most one-year periods you made money; in some you lost.

---

[38] To dredge up your high school statistics, volatility is usually measured by the *standard deviation* of returns. People use different time periods and intervals to calculate standard deviations so the numbers you might see aren't always comparable.

On average you made about 12%. Very nice. But in one out of five yearly periods you lost, sometimes a lot. The worst was February 2009, when you lost 43% of what you had the year before. If you needed your money at that time, you would have been very unhappy. That's risk. Here's a picture.

S&P 500 One-Year Return

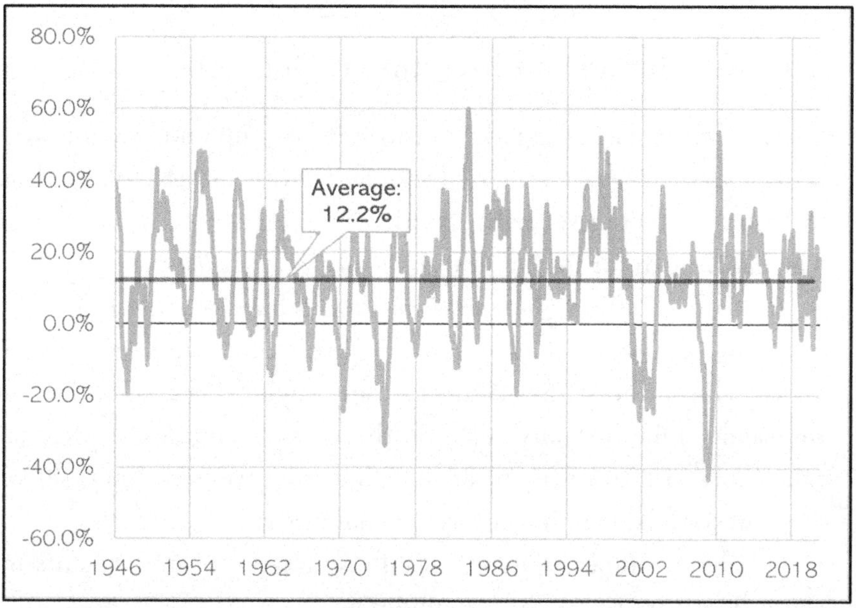

Eggs, Baskets, Etc.

In the past, the stock market has always recovered from losses. You did okay if you hung in long enough. The same is not true for individual company stocks. Companies often go out of business or get bought by other companies when their stock prices are down. In fact, half of all companies don't last more than seven years in the stock market.[39] Problem is, you don't know which half.

[39] Henrik Bessembinder, "Do Stocks Outperform Treasury Bills?", Journal of Financial Economics, Vol 129, Issue 3, September 2018.

Fortunately, there is a simple way to deal with the risk of owning loser stocks: make sure you own winners as well. In other words, own a lot of stocks. Even better, own them all. This is called not putting all your eggs in one basket, or *diversification*. The quip is that "diversification is the only free lunch on Wall Street."[40] Thanks to mutual funds and ETFs, and specifically index funds, it is very easy and cheap to diversify your investments.

The Most Important Investment Decision[41]

The stock market is risky because it goes up and down a lot. To reduce risk, you put less in stocks and more in less volatile bonds, inflation-protected securities, and cash (i.e., your savings account). The fancy term for finding the right mix is *asset allocation*.

Figuring out the right asset allocation is *the* most important part of investing. For the last several years, investors have been in a tough spot. The interest available in safe savings accounts has been miniscule. Like basically zero. So there has been a lot of pressure to take more risk in order to have a shot at more investment income. The question is, can they afford to take this risk.

It helps to think about when different types of investments make sense. Here are some general guidelines.

Stocks: Stocks are good when you want to build wealth over a period of five or more years *but* you can live with the possibility of ending up with less. Stocks of American companies should be your mainstay. Consider adding some international stocks, both from more developed economies such as Japan, the United Kingdom, and Germany, and faster-growing, "emerging markets" such as China and Brazil. The reason is that different countries' markets do well at different times.

---

[40] The quote is attributed to economist Harry Markowitz.

[41] All fund information in this section from company websites as of 2/16/2020

TIPS or I-Bonds: For far-off goals, such as retirement, put some savings into inflation-protected securities. This is your "safe" money. It won't grow a lot more than inflation, but we've seen that over longer periods the risk that inflation will eat away at the value of your savings is significant. TIPS and I-Bonds are guaranteed to keep up.

CDs: These super-charged savings accounts are for when you absolutely, positively need your money to be there at a certain point in the future. CDs are best for periods up to about five years. You can pick the date you need the money and know in advance exactly how much interest you will earn.

Bonds: Intermediate or long-term bonds (bonds that mature in four or more years) can pay a little more interest than CDs for goals that are more than five years in the future. They fluctuate in value, but much less than stocks. Very short-term bonds (bonds that mature in one to three years) don't fluctuate as much and can be used to "park" some money and perhaps earn just a bit more than in a savings account.

So much for generalities. What is the right asset allocation *for you*? I'm going to give you three options for preparing your personal asset allocation.

1. Asset Allocation – Stovetop Recipe

You can use the **worksheet** on this book's website to figure out your asset allocation. Enter your goals, how much you've saved to date, and when you need the money. Then think about the four questions below and decide how you might allocate the savings for each goal.

- What is the time horizon of this goal? When do I need the money?
- Can I achieve it just by saving or do I need a lot of investment income to get there?
- How flexible is the goal? Can I postpone it or do with less if I invest more in stocks and they go down?

- How much of a risk taker am I? Will I be able to sleep at night if my wealth goes down 10%? 20%? 30%?

The sheet will calculate your total asset allocation as shown in the example on the facing page. As a bonus (not shown) it calculates *how much more you need to save* each month to reach your goal. That depends not just on your asset allocation but also on the return you expect each type of investment to deliver. Assume a higher return and you need to save less, but the risk of falling short increases. The returns in the sheet are expected *real* returns [42]. You can substitute your own or those of your favorite forecaster. Just don't let yourself off the saving hook by assuming unrealistic returns.

Once you've landed on an asset allocation, you need to take your savings and invest. I'm going to list some specific ETFs and mutual funds that are good candidates in each of the major asset classes described above.

The main criteria I used to select these funds are *broad diversification* and *low expenses*. Broad diversification to avoid ending up with too many losers and not enough winners in any given asset class, and low expenses so you get to keep as much of the return on your investments as possible.

I apologize if this gets weedy, but if you want to implement the concepts from this chapter you do need to know what specific investments to buy.

---

[42] *Real* returns are what you expect to earn over and above inflation. To get *"nominal"* returns that *include* inflation add the inflation rate to each real return. I assumed future inflation to be 1.7% a year.

The truth is that market forecasts are guesses clothed in more or less elaborate financial models. But you have to assume *something*. The numbers in the worksheet are derived from AQR for stocks; TIPS and bond yields from the Federal Reserve Bank of St. Louis; and CD and savings rates from Bankrate.com; all as of January 2020.

Asset Allocation Worksheet

				Asset Allocation				
Purpose/goal	**Amount needed**	**Amount saved**	**When needed** (# of years)	Grow my money but risk loss **% Stocks**	Need guaranteed amount **% CDs**	Protect against inflation **% TIPS / I-Bonds**	Extra interest with some risk **% Bonds**	Available savings **% Cash**
Enter your assumed return for each asset class in this row >>				4.70%	0.50%	0.20%	0.70%	0.00%
Replace specific goals with your own below				**Enter asset allocation for each goal below**				
Buy a car	$8,000	$6,000	2	0%	0%	0%	50%	50%
Home down payment	$30,000	$12,000	5	25%	25%	25%	25%	0%
Retirement fund	$1,000,000	$20,000	30	80%	0%	20%	0%	0%
Total Allocation in $	**$1,038,000**	**$38,000**		**$19,000**	**$3,000**	**$7,000**	**$6,000**	**$3,000**
Total Allocation in %				**50%**	**8%**	**18%**	**16%**	**8%**

The first table below lists ETFs, which means you can buy them in any regular or IRA brokerage account. ETFs are generally not available in employer retirement plans or 529 college savings plans.

Asset Class	Fund Name (funds in each asset class are comparable; choose any one)	Ticker Symbol	Expense Ratio
U.S. stocks	Vanguard Total Stock Market ETF	**VTI**	0.03%
	Schwab U.S. Broad Market ETF	**SCHB**	0.03%
	iShares Core S&P Total U.S. Stock Market ETF	**ITOT**	0.03%
International stocks	Vanguard Total International Stock ETF	**VXUS**	0.09%
	iShares Core MSCI Total International Stock ETF	**IXUS**	0.09%
TIPS	Schwab U.S. TIPS ETF	**SCHP**	0.05%
Bonds	Vanguard Total Bond Market ETF	**BND**	0.035%
	Schwab U.S. Aggregate Bond ETF	**SCHZ**	0.04%
	iShares Core U.S. Aggregate Bond ETF	**AGG**	0.05%

Vanguard's ETFs are also available as mutual funds. Either way you own the same underlying stocks and bonds. You can buy mutual funds directly on Vanguard's site without opening a brokerage account, but you have to invest at least $3,000 per fund. You might also find them offered in your 401(k) or 529 plans, sometimes with the alternate ticker symbols below.

ETF	Vanguard Mutual Fund	Mutual Fund Ticker Symbols	Expense Ratio
VTI	Total Stock Market Index Fund	**VTSAX** (VITNX, VSMPX)	0.04%
VXUS	Total International Stock Index Fund	**VITNX** (VTSNX, VTPSX)	0.11%
BND	Total Bond Market Index Fund	**VBTLX** (VBTIX, VBMPX)	0.05%
SCHP	Inflation Protected Securities Fund	**VIPSX** (VAIPX, VIPIX)	0.20%

I suggest putting 60% to 75% of your stock investments in the U.S. market. Any one of the funds listed in this category is a good choice. The remainder of your stocks should be in international stocks. Again, any of the funds listed will do the trick.

The easiest way to buy inflation-protected securities is through the Schwab TIPS ETFs. There are also TIPS mutual funds and I've listed one from Vanguard. I recommend mutual funds for retirement accounts. If you're enterprising you can even buy individual TIPS in a brokerage account. (Diversifying is not necessary with TIPS, since they are all issued by the government.)

For non-retirement accounts, I am a big fan of buying I-Bonds through **www.treasurydirect.gov**. Like TIPS, I-Bonds are not about earning a high return. They are about protecting some of your savings against inflation. I-Bonds are under-appreciated for several reasons: you don't have to pay tax on the interest until you cash in the bond (which can be as long as thirty years), you can cash it in at any time after a year without having to worry about the value going down, and you're protected against *both* inflation *and* deflation.

What about CDs? The best way is to shop around for the highest interest rates available on sites such as **Bankrate.com**. In most cases they will be available either as a regular, taxable certificate or as an IRA. You can buy some CDs through your accounts at Schwab or Fidelity as well. This is simple, but you may not get as good a deal.

2. Asset Allocation – Microwave Instructions

Don't have the time or patience to go through the asset allocation stovetop recipe? Here's a better-than-nothing short cut. Use **a risk tolerance questionnaire** from a firm like Vanguard to determine a stock-bond mix that fits your objectives. Then choose a corresponding fund that invests in and maintains your stock-bond mix. Here are some options.

Fund Family	Available Mix (% stocks/% bonds and cash)	Expense ratio
Vanguard Life Strategy Mutual Funds	20/80; 40/60; 60/40; 80/20	0.13%
iShares Core Allocation ETFs	30/70; 40/60; 60/40; 80/20	0.25%
Fidelity Asset Manager Mutual Funds	20/80; 30/70; 40/60; 50/50; 60/40; 70/30; 85/15	0.53% - 0.74%

My reservation about these instant meals is that they do not put much money to TIPS. Instead, almost all of the bonds are "nominal," which is bad if inflation jumps unexpectedly.

3. Asset Allocation – Happy Meal

Still too much for you? There's an even simpler approach to asset allocation that's based just on your expected retirement date (or, in the case of 529 college savings accounts, the college enrollment date): *target date funds*. These are one-size-fits-all, but they are still far better than letting your savings flounder haplessly in the hinterland. Many 401(k) and 403(b) plans automatically invest your contributions in target date funds, which is good.

Target date funds usually have a future year in their names. For example, the Fidelity Freedom 2050 Index Fund is meant for people who plan to retire around 2050. When the target year is far in the future, the funds will mostly be invested in stocks. As it draws closer, the mix shifts more toward bonds. As an example, here is the planned mix of the Fidelity Freedom Index Funds.

Fidelity Target Date Fund Asset Allocation

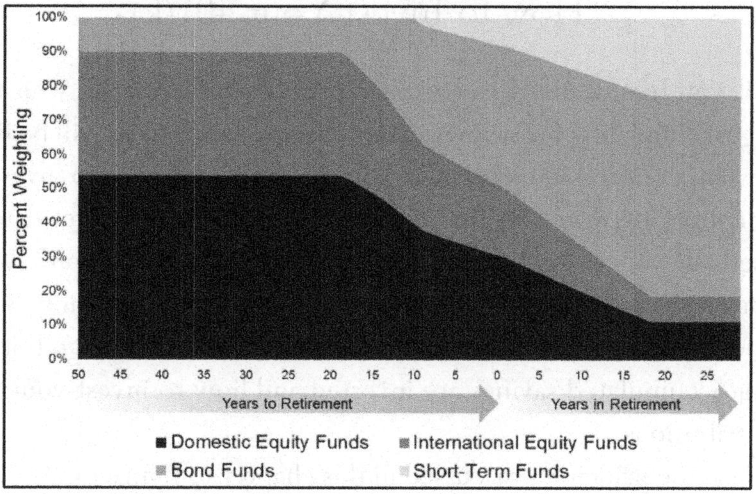

Source: Fidelity Freedom Index Fund Summary Prospectus as of 5/30/2019

Here are target date fund options. Both Fidelity and Schwab have two series of funds with similar names. Make sure to use the *index* fund series, which have lower expense ratios.

Fund Family	Target Dates	Expense Ratio
Schwab Target Date Index Funds	Every 5 years 2010 – 2060	0.08%
Fidelity Freedom Index Funds	Every 5 years 2005 - 2065	0.12%
Vanguard Target Retirement Funds	Every 5 years 2015 – 2065	0.13%

How to Invest Your 401(k)

If you have a 401(k) or similar plan at work, it may well be the biggest chunk of your savings. Your investment options will be limited to what's offered in the plan. If you never elected how to invest your contributions, you may find that your money is in a target date fund based on your age. You could do worse. What you don't want is having it sit in a money market fund earning next to nothing. So it's a good idea to review your asset allocation. You can change both how your accumulated savings are invested and how to invest your future contributions.

Use the principles discussed in this chapter to figure out what asset allocation makes sense for you. Choose funds with low expense ratios where possible, which will often be from companies such as *Vanguard*, *Fidelity*, and *Dimensional Fund Advisors (DFA)*. Index funds tend to be the lowest cost. Don't pay attention to how funds did in the past; it does not predict how they will do in the future. Some plans offer a rainbow of options. Don't be tempted to sample everything. Like colors, mixing more than two or three funds quickly leaves you just with brown. Keep it simple.

Your Investment Plan

Once you have determined your asset allocation and how you will invest, *write it down*.[43] One page is all you need. Having it on paper will help you remember, stay the course, and avoid making impulsive decisions.

---

[43] This kind of document comes with a fancy name, *Investment Policy Statement (IPS)*, but it doesn't need to be fancy. Every investor large and small should have one.

Following is what a plan might look like (Chapter 26 explains the reference to "ESG" funds):

Example of a Written Investment Plan

Jane Doe Investment Plan As of January 1, 2020	
Goals and time horizon	I am investing to buy a used car in two years, make a down payment on an apartment in 5 years, and retire when I turn 67
Attitude toward risk	I am uncomfortable taking a lot of risk with my money, but I recognize that I have to accept the chance of losing some in order to achieve my goals
Target asset allocation	Overall, I will allocate my current savings 50% in stocks / 50% in bonds, TIPS, and CDs. My retirement money will be allocated 80% in stocks and 20% in TIPS or I-Bonds. My stocks will be 65% in U.S. stocks and 35% foreign stocks
Accounts	For retirement savings I will save as much as possible in my employer's 401(k) and in IRA or Roth IRA accounts. For other savings, I will invest in CDs and a taxable brokerage account
Investments	I will buy low-cost index funds (either ETFs or mutual funds) whenever possible. In my 401(k) I will use a target date fund and a TIPS fund
Rebalancing	I will revisit my goals and asset allocation once a year and update them as needed
Special considerations	I will choose ESG funds where I have the option. In his memory I will hold on to the 20 shares of Coca Cola stock that I inherited from my grandfather

Rebalancing

If you cook your own asset allocation you should *rebalance* periodically. This simply means recalculating your actual allocation, comparing it to your target, and adjusting if necessary. For example, assume your target for stocks is 50%. If stocks plunge, your total portfolio will go down, but stocks may end up being just 45% of the lower total. Bonds (or other assets) will now be above target. So you sell some bonds and buy stocks to get back to target. Through this book's website you can access a simple **worksheet** to calculate how much to buy and sell.

Why rebalance? It keeps your portfolio from becoming riskier or less risky just because of market moves. In normal times, rebalancing once a year is enough. When there are large market moves it makes sense to check in quarterly. Don't overdo it. If you're within 5% of your target allocation it's fine to leave things alone.

One benefit of asset allocation funds (the microwave recipe) and target date funds (the happy meal) is that they do the rebalancing for you automatically. You literally don't need to look at your portfolio for years—and that can be a very good thing.

Chapter 15: Money in Your Head

Brian Fantana: "They've done studies you know. Sixty percent of the time it works every time."

– Anchorman: The Legend of Ron Burgundy (2004)

In the middle of the last century some smart economists came up with mathematical models to figure out the "best" way to invest. In these models investors were totally rational. They didn't do stupid things. The math in the models was hard, which made the economists happy. They called their invention "modern portfolio theory" and were awarded Nobel prizes for it.[44]

Some decades later another group of smart professors came along and said "Wait...people aren't rational at all." They found that we humans have lots of "irrational" biases. Here are some examples of what they found: Most people would rather avoid losing $10 than win $10, even if the chances of winning are higher. When people make decisions, they tend to give more weight to recent experiences than longer-ago ones. People tend to accept facts which confirm their existing beliefs and reject those which contradict them. And many

---

[44] The previously mentioned Harry Markowitz is often considered the inventor of "modern portfolio theory". Other luminaries include William Sharpe, inventor of a famous model called the "capital asset pricing model", and Eugene Fama who is credited with the "efficient market hypothesis." All three received Nobel prizes for their work

more. The professors became known as "behavioralists" and they too got some Nobel prizes.[45]

Why am I going on about this? Because being human can get in the way of making smart money decisions. We've already talked about ways to automate saving, control credit card use, and use a budget to keep spending in check. It's just as important to avoid impulsive decisions when investing.

Say you invest in the stock market in order to accumulate a retirement kitty twenty years from now. Because stocks are tied to the economy they have gone up on average. In fact, there has never been a 20-year period where the stocks didn't make money, even after inflation. Knowing this, maybe you shouldn't really worry if the stock market bounces around in the interim. But will you have the stomach to weather the ups and downs?

As I write this in early 2020, investors are being tested. Say you diligently spent ten years putting away $500 a month into your 401(k) and invested it in the stock market. You've earned a respectable 8% return on average, which means you have accumulated a total of $91,500. Nice. $100,000 seems within reach.

On February 21, 2020 you wake up and concern about the coronavirus is growing. The market drops three days in a row and your balance is down to $84,700. You tell yourself you're in it for the long term and carry on. The market bounces around over the next eight days, with big one-day swings up and down. On March 9th, there's another big drop; your balance is now $74,500. Should you maybe move your money into something safer to preserve what you have left? After all, you just lost almost three years of saving $500 a month in the space of three weeks. You decide to keep the faith. Another few days of wild swings and on March 16th the market drops

[45] The first type of "irrational" behavior is known as "loss aversion," the second as "recency bias," and the third as "confirmation bias." Daniel Kahnemann and Richard Thaler are among the pioneers of what has become known as "behavioral economics." Both received Nobel Prizes.

another 12%. By the end of the week your balance is $62,500. Thirty-two percent of your account. Up in thin air. In just one month. On Facebook your friends are talking about how they "got out" just in time. You feel like an idiot.[46]

What do you do? Will the market lose another 30% or will it rebound? Nobody knows. It's ironic but true: in investments you are tempted to sell when things are cheaper and buy when they are more expensive.

The challenge in this situation—and it's a formidable challenge—is to swallow hard and continue saving and investing (buying). In the past, the stock market has always recovered—sometimes in a matter of months, but sometimes only after many years. You don't know whether this will be true in the future. There is a chance that it won't be. But one thing is certain: if you're not invested, it *definitely* won't be true for your portfolio.

(Of course if your earnings picture has changed—for example, if you're at risk of losing your job, you may need to reassess your goals, potentially boosting your emergency fund first.)

In a scenario such as this, let inertia work for you. One way to reduce the impulse to sell is to remove the stimulus: *stop looking at your account balance*. This is good advice even during normal times. There is no reason to look at your investment balances more than once a quarter or even once a year when your goal is years or decades in the future. Long-term investing can be really boring. You can go for years without doing anything and be wildly successful. The temptation is to futz around with your investments, buy a little of this, sell a little of that. Avoid tinkering just to "do something." This is why having your portfolio on your phone is a bad idea. Apps such as Robinhood, which "gamify" trading, can be dangerous to long-term investing success.

[46] These are actual market changes in 2020 (applied to the made-up balance of $91,500). It turned out the market rebounded shortly thereafter.

Inertia is also your friend when it comes to saving, and in particular retirement plan contributions. Set up your 401(k) to invest and go away. You'll automatically buy more stocks when the market is down and fewer when it is strong—without making any conscious decision.

Trading Bugs

Every now and then a new crop of young Turks discovers the stock market. Often it happens when the market looks like it's got nowhere to go but up. But not always: the COVID-19 crisis is the latest example. Apparently people got bored, they were sitting at home, there were no sports to bet on, so they started trading stocks. Exhibit one: the wild ride of GameStop and other "meme" stocks in February of 2021.

Pandemic or not, what if it happens to you? You're getting the hang of this financial stuff. It's kinda cool. Maybe you have a great stock idea? A guaranteed-to-win option strategy? Here's my advice: keep your financial future on track when scratching that itch. Give yourself a budget to work with. Set up a separate brokerage account that can be your "sandbox" for making bets on the market. As long as you don't have a gambling disorder and are prepared to lose this money, have at it. But do not dip into your retirement fund to do it.

Chapter 16: Shared Money

Charlie: "I'm leaving the country, Mitch. I need a fake passport and I need money, lots of it."

Mitch Henessey: "Well why didn't you say so? Hold on a minute while I pull that outta my ass."

– The Long Kiss Goodnight (1996)

Whether you have a roommate, are taking in a family member, moving in with a partner, or are just out with some friends, a time will come when you want to share money in some way, e.g., split expenses, investments, or even debts. This can be good, because sharing costs can make things possible that otherwise might not be, such as paying rent in an expensive city, splitting a vacation, starting a business.

Shared financial benefits come in other ways as well, for example when one partner stays home to avoid the cost of outside childcare, when an employer offers health insurance that covers both partners, or when two incomes are needed to get a mortgage.

But money can also cause problems in relationships. You may not have the same attitudes about spending, goals and priorities, or the value of monetary versus non-monetary contributions. Different opinions about what each person is contributing and what is "fair" can lead to tensions that build up gradually and erupt if there is a financial crunch.

Communication

The first step when beginning a shared financial life should be to have a conversation about how the sharing will occur. Which expenses will be shared? How much is each person responsible for? How will you deal with unexpected costs? What if one person loses their income? Don't assume agreement without having the conversation. Don't assume your view of what is "fair" is the same as others'.

Especially when you don't know the other person(s) well, recognize that they may be uncomfortable about disclosing their finances. They may not want to talk about debts or other financial obligations, spending habits, or even addictions. If they are wealthy, they may be self-conscious about that too; don't assume everyone who has money wants to brag or broadcast it. Avoid being judgmental and focus on the parts of your financial lives that are shared. But also make sure you get enough info to know they will be good for their share of expenses.

For partners and spouses, the necessary questions extend beyond spending. How will existing and future assets be shared? Will you own things jointly or separately? What about debt? Who will be responsible for paying existing and future debts?

Keeping Track

A good second step when sharing money is to create a budget of shared expenses that lays out each person's contribution. For example, if you have roommates, will you split rent evenly or do some pay more because they have a nicer room? Will you share expenses for food regardless of relative appetites? Some expenses probably won't be shared, like haircuts, gym memberships, and student loan payments.

One approach is to open a separate checking account from which common expenses are paid. Each person contributes their monthly budgeted amount to the account. Or check out **Splitwise**, an app specifically destined to make splitting expenses easy.

Couples might choose to comingle their finances more or less. Will you keep separate checking accounts, a joint account, or both? What about investment accounts? Separate or joint? (Some accounts have to be separate, such as retirement accounts and HSAs.) Consider a budget app designed specifically for couples such as **Zeta** or **Honeyfi**.

When it comes to credit cards, consider having each partner as a primary account owner on at least one card to build and maintain independent credit scores. Recognize, however, if you have joint responsibility for certain payments, such as a mortgage or rent, both scores will be affected by missed payments.

Joint Responsibilities

Often shared financial relationships start when there is good will all around. You're dealing with friends or family; you want things to be good; you don't want to think about money fights. Unfortunately, sometimes relationships sour. Be aware of some of the legal implications:

- If you co-sign or guarantee a lease or a loan, you are responsible for full payment no matter what happens.
- If you own an asset jointly—a home, a car—it may not be easy to "take your half" in the event of a split.
- If you own a bank account jointly, either owner can empty it at any time.
- In community property states [47], any debt that either of you incurs *while married* is your joint responsibility. Likewise, any property either of you acquires while married belongs to both of you equally. Debts and assets from before you were married

---

[47] Arizona, California, Idaho, Louisiana, Nevada, New Mexico, Texas, Washington, and Wisconsin.

aren't usually considered community property. If you divorce, each of you gets and owes half. In other states, an even split is not a given—a judge might determine a different split is equitable.

Chapter 17: Uncle Sam's Money

Nathan Arizona, Sr: "All right, boy, I guess you got a reward coming. Twenty-five thousand dollars. Or, if you need home furnishings, I can give you a line of credit at any of my stores. In fact, that's the way I'd rather handle it. Tax reasons."

– Raising Arizona (1987)

This book is not a tax guide, for which you should thank me. But taxes are a big deal when it comes to your financial life, so I'm going to go over a few practical considerations and important concepts.

Practical Tax Stuff

Here are some non-optional things to know about income taxes.

Deadlines

In the beginning there was the deadline: *April 15th* of every year.[48] Burn this date into your memory. Missing the deadline means hassles and penalties. If you are self-employed there are also quarterly dates (June 15th, September 15th, January 15th, in addition to April 15th) because you may need to make quarterly tax payments. And just

---

[48] The date gets pushed out if April 15th falls in a weekend or holiday. You can also receive an automatic extension to October 15th, but this is for filing the return only. Any taxes you owe must still be paid by April 15th.

because there is a deadline does not mean you should wait until the last minute. File early.

What do you file?

You file separate income *tax returns* with the federal government (the Internal Revenue Service or IRS) and each state you lived or earned money in during the previous year. For example, if you lived in one state and worked in another, you will need to file two state tax returns.[49] A tax return takes the income you earned and grinds it through a series of formulas to figure how much tax you owe. If more tax was withheld from your pay (or you paid more in quarterly payments) than you owe, you receive a tax refund. If not, you have to make up the difference.

Do you have to file?

Probably. You *should* file a return if you worked and your employer took federal or state income taxes out of your paycheck since you might get money back. You *have to* file once you earn more than a certain amount (which varies depending on whether you're single or married, or have kids). There are also other circumstances under which you *must* file, including if you made more than $400 from self-employment.

How to file?

In most cases, you'll want to file your taxes electronically. First, figure out whether you can file for free with the **IRS** and check out the filing options on your state website(s). The programs recommended by the IRS are versions of commercial programs. If you don't qualify for free filing, you'll be charged a fee based on how complicated your return is.

---

[49] A handful of states don't have income taxes: Alaska, Florida, Nevada, South Dakota, Texas, Washington, and Wyoming. And most states don't make you pay taxes on income on which you've paid taxes to another state.

There is no single best program, but **TurboTax**, **H&R Block**, and **TaxAct** are all relatively user-friendly. They may try to lure you into paying extra for more expensive versions or sell you other services. Often you can get even complex returns done without upgrading.

If you sign up with **Credit Karma**—the free credit score website—you can file your taxes for free even if your income is higher and your situation more complicated. The downside is that you agree to be bombarded with financial offers.

On-line programs save your tax return information on their servers (somewhere in the cloud). They're expected to have similar security as banks to protect your information. As an alternative, you can *buy* the software from some of the companies. When you do, completing your return is similar to the online versions but the information is stored on your own computer.

What if you want help? Depending on your situation you may be able to have your taxes prepared for free by volunteer preparers as part of the IRS's **VITA/TCE** program. Otherwise, you need to go to a professional: this should be a *certified public accountant (CPA)* licensed in your state or an *Enrolled Agent* certified by the IRS. You should expect to pay in the $175-$350 range unless you have a complicated situation.

If you are due a refund be prepared to provide one or more bank account numbers to have the money deposited directly: it's faster and more secure than a check.

When do I get my refund?

Your federal refund usually comes in less than three weeks after you file if you selected direct deposit. You can check your refund status at the IRS's **website**.

Do not take the bait if you're offered "instant" refunds or tax refund loans by your tax preparer or software. Even if loans are marketed as "zero interest," you'll probably be paying a high effective rate through tax preparation charges or other fees. See the chapter on debt if you need emergency money.

Important Tax Concepts

Here are some common tax concepts that often cause confusion.

Tax Rates

Sometimes, believe it or not, people worry about making *too much* money. Specifically, they're concerned about "moving into a higher tax bracket." The implication is that this somehow leaves them less well off. Not.

Tax brackets use *marginal tax rates.* A marginal tax rate is the tax rate you have to pay on the next dollar you earn. Below is a picture of the federal income tax brackets for a single individual in 2020. (Most years, tax brackets go up slightly for inflation.)

Tax Brackets for Single Filers

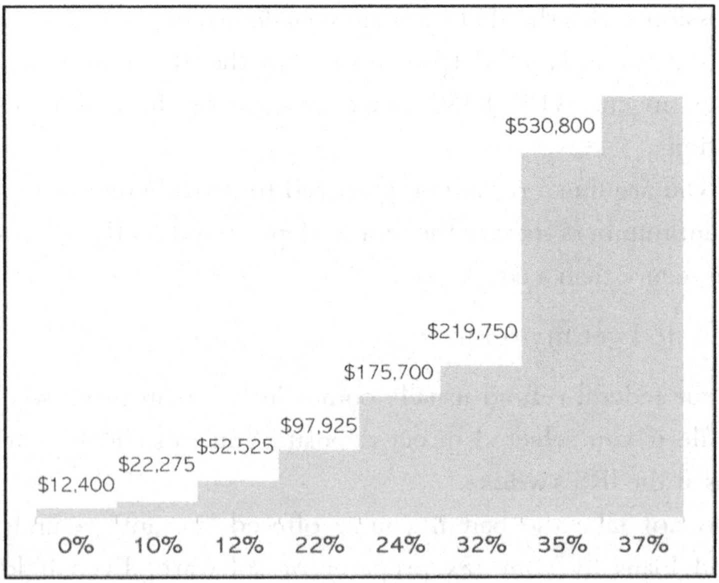

Notice that nobody pays tax on the first $12,400 they make. Everybody pays 10% tax on the next $9,875. After that, the next $30,250 is taxed at 12%. And so on. Somebody making $60,000 has a marginal tax rate of 22% because that is the rate an additional dollar of income would be taxed at.[50]

Not to be confused with marginal tax rates is the *average tax rate*, sometimes also called the *effective tax rate*. This takes the total taxes owed divided by income. The person making $60,000 pays tax of $12,400 x 0% + $9,875 x 10% + $30,250 x 12% + $7,475 x 22%, which comes out to total tax of $6,262 or an average/effective tax rate of 10.4%.

The takeaway: you may pay a higher marginal tax rate if you make more and move into a higher tax bracket, but you are still better off.[51]

Types of Income

The type of income you earn affects your tax rate. This becomes important as your net worth grows and you start earning investment income.

Ordinary income is income taxed at (so-called ordinary) tax rates such as those shown above for a single filer. It includes income from work and other sources such pensions, interest, rental income, and gambling winnings.

Some *investment income* is taxed at lower rates. Many stock dividends and long-term capital gains are taxed at a top rate of 15% for most people (20% if you're rich).

---

[50] This is simplified. The actual "taxable income" to which the rate is applied involves a number of calculations that you go through when filing a return. Taxable income is usually lower than your gross income.

[51] With taxes, there's always a "but." There are a few areas of the tax code that can raise your marginal tax rate to more than 100%, meaning you pay more in extra tax than the extra income. The most common are related to various credits that phase out as income increases.

Deductions vs. Credits

Another common confusion is between tax deductions and tax credits. In general, credits are better than deductions.

Tax deductions reduce the income used to calculate how much tax you owe. If your marginal tax rate is 15%, a one-dollar tax deduction saves you 15 cents in taxes. Contributions to 401(k) plans, IRAs, and HSAs are deductible, as is interest paid on student loans, up to certain limits. On top of these, you generally choose either a *standard deduction* that is a fixed amount, or you elect to *itemize deductions*. You choose the option that reduces your income (and hence your tax bill) the most.

Tax credits reduce your tax bill directly. A one-dollar tax credit reduces your tax bill by one dollar, regardless of your tax rate. Some tax credits are *refundable*, meaning that even if you don't owe any tax, you will receive a refund for the amount of the credit. The Earned Income Tax Credit or EITC is one of the most significant refundable credits for people with low to middle incomes who work, especially if they have children.

Tax Planning

It's complicated. But it can put real money in your pocket. Instead of tinkering with your portfolio to eke out questionable gains spend some time understanding taxes.

Resources

Government and Regulatory Agencies		
IRS.gov	Tax documentation and publications	**https://www.irs.gov/**
	Verify whether your tax preparer is an Enrolled Agent (does not include CPAs)	**https://www.irs.gov/tax-professionals/verify-the-status-of-an-enrolled-agent**

Chapter 18: Money in Retirement

Shelby Eatenton Latcherie: "The money is real nice and all. But I just like the idea of growing old with somebody. My dream is to get old, and sit on the back porch, covered with grandchildren, and I'll say: 'No!' and 'Stop that!'"

– Steel Magnolias (1989)

When you're in your twenties and thirties you may not be dreaming of porches. But we saw in the chapter on compounding returns how powerful an ally *time* is when it comes to saving money. And time you only get once.

That's why there is one overarching piece of advice about retirement: start putting away as big a chunk of money every month *as early as you can*. Find an asset allocation that will let you sleep at night, and then leave it alone.

Retirement used to be a three-legged stool for many workers: Social Security, a pension, and savings. Things are wobblier today. More people have to rely on Social Security and savings alone. Pensions—also known as *defined benefit* plans—are becoming less common. Instead, 401(k) and other *defined contribution* plans have shifted the burden of saving and the risk of investing to workers. Even where pensions still exist there often is a big gap between the benefits that were promised and the money set aside to pay them. This problem of "underfunded pensions" has many people worried that the promised payments are in jeopardy.

Social Security

As we saw in Chapter 3, if you work you pay Social Security tax. Paying this tax entitles you to receive benefits when you retire. You can work on and off, but you need at least ten years under your belt to get any benefits. How much you get will be based on your average earnings over thirty-five years. Say you average $60,000 of income a year over that period; then you can expect to receive a yearly benefit of about $26,000. If you're married, your spouse gets at least another $13,000 even if they didn't work at all. Also, Social Security benefits are at least partially tax-free, so they go a bit further than regular earnings.

There are two major advantages of Social Security. One is that benefits increase with inflation. The dollar figures here are for 2020, but they will increase with future inflation. The second is that benefits last for life. You'll get monthly checks even if you live to be 100 or more.

When do you start getting benefits? Full retirement age for anyone born after 1960 is sixty-seven. You can start collecting as early as sixty-two, but you'll get much less. You can also opt to delay benefits until you are seventy and get significantly more. For most healthy people, planning to delay is a smart move. Of course, that means working longer or having other money to live on until age seventy.

Will Social Security be there when you are ready to retire? Right now, the cushion ("trust fund") built up in the past is being used up and expected to run out by 2034. At that point, FICA taxes paid by workers are expected to only cover about 76% of promised benefits. No one knows how Congress will deal with this. Either benefits will be reduced, or the government needs to raise taxes or borrow more.

Most likely it will be some combination of the three. But it is unlikely that benefits will disappear entirely.

It's not too early to set up a **my Social Security** account, which will let you check your earnings history for accuracy, estimate your future benefits, get a replacement Social Security card, and more.

Savings

With Social Security alone, you probably won't be able to maintain your pre-retirement standard of living. That's why taking advantage of retirement saving incentives (see Chapter 10) should be part of your plan.

How much do you need to save? It obviously depends upon what kind of a beach you want to retire on. Here is an important perspective. Focus on how much extra income you want in retirement and work backwards. The table below gives a rough rule of thumb for how big a pile of money will give you that income.[52]

Desired Annual Income	Savings Target		
	Conservative (pretty likely to be enough)	Moderate (should suffice)	Aggressive (can last with a little luck)
$10,000	$330,000	$250,000	$220,000
$25,000	$830,000	$625,000	$550,000
$40,000	$1,330,000	$1,000,000	$890,000
$75,000	$2,500,000	$1,875,000	$1,665,000

[52] These are high-level estimates based on common "withdrawal rates" of 3%, 4%, and 4.5% respectively. There is lots of research on withdrawal rates and many tools to refine the calculations. If you're approaching retirement, it might be worth having a financial planner crunch some numbers for you.

These numbers should be an eye opener and reinforce the message at the beginning of the chapter: *Let time work for you and start saving for retirement right away.*

Annuities

As you get older, you may become a target for annuity salespeople. Annuities are bewildering financial products. They are often rightfully slammed for being too complicated and expensive. Unfortunately, they are also often pushed onto unsuspecting seniors.

There are two types of annuities to keep on your radar: *immediate annuities* and *deferred income annuities*. They protect you against *longevity risk*, which is the risk of living so long that you run out of savings. It *may* make sense to buy one of these with some of your retirement savings to ensure that you have at least some money coming in for the rest of your life.

Immediate Annuities

With an immediate annuity you hand over a chunk of money to an insurance company and in return you get a guaranteed monthly payment for the rest of your life, starting immediately. Think of this as a permanent, irreversible deal. If you die early, you will have bought insurance against living too long that you didn't need. But if you live super long, the annuity has you covered.[53]

Deferred Income or Longevity Annuities (DIAs)

DIAs work like immediate annuities, but you give the insurance company money today and payments start sometime in the future—usually ten to twenty years later. The payments from a DIA are proportionately much higher than from an immediate annuity. DIAs

---

[53] There are optional features that guarantee you get some minimum amount, but you get lower regular payments.

are intended to make sure you have money coming in if you grow really old. Don't confuse DIAs with various *deferred annuities* such as fixed annuities, fixed indexed annuities, or variable annuities, which are the complicated, expensive ones. With a DIA you know today the size of the payment you will receive starting at a predetermined, advanced age.

Buying Annuities

The insurance company you get the annuity from should be financially strong. Even though there are some state protections for consumers, you want this company to be around for decades. There are several *rating agencies* that analyze the financial strength of insurance companies; the main ones are *Standard and Poor's*, *Moody's*, and *A.M. Best*. Buy annuities only from a company that has very strong ratings from Standard and Poor's (AA or better) or Moody's (Aa2 or better). You can usually find financial strength ratings on the insurance company's website. **New York Life** is one of the highest rated companies and often has competitive quotes. Other strong annuity companies are **Mass Mutual** and **Guardian Life**.

It's also usually best to get a so-called "life" annuity. This is one that pays you until you (and your spouse, if it is a "joint life") die and then stops. You might see options such as a "period certain" or "refund at death" which guarantee some further payments if you die relatively early. But usually they are not worth the lower regular payments.

Annuities can give you some peace of mind in retirement. Be aware, though, that unlike Social Security, the payments aren't guaranteed to keep up with inflation.

You buy annuities through an insurance agent. One source for quotes is online insurance agency **Blueprint Income**. Schwab and Fidelity have affiliated insurance agencies that can also provide quotes. Note though, that regardless of the agency you buy from, it's the insurance company that makes and guarantees the payments.

Resources

Government and Regulatory Agencies		
Social Security Administration	All things Social Security, with information and calculators	https://www.ssa.gov/
	Overview brochure on Social Security and Medicare	https://www.ssa.gov/pubs/EN-05-10035.pdf

Businesses		
Open Social Security	Good free calculator by a CPA and long-time financial blogger to figure out when to claim Social Security	https://opensocialsecurity.com/

Chapter 19: Money Left Behind

Immortan Joe: "You will ride eternal, shiny and chrome."

– Mad Max: Fury Road (2015)

Life sneaks up on you. If you're saving and investing you may find yourself sooner rather than later with a respectable net worth. Or you become a parent and now you have to think about the future of your child(ren) should something happen to you. Responsibility and entanglements pile up. Even if you're not hurtling toward the gates of Valhalla it's time to put in place a basic *estate plan*.

What is an estate plan? It's a plan to control what happens if you're no longer able to make important decisions. Estate plans are a turn-off because they force you to think about...you know...*death*. Worse, you may have to work with a lawyer to put one together. It's no wonder that 60% of adults don't have one.[54] None of this is an excuse for waiting.

[54] According to a 2017 survey by Caring.com

Why You Shouldn't Wait to Create an Estate Plan

Who will care for your minor child(ren) if you die or become incapacitated?

If you have children under the age of eighteen, you should appoint a legal guardian, someone who you trust will care for them if you are no longer able to. If you don't appoint a guardian in writing, generally as part of a *Last Will and Testament*, the state will appoint someone and that someone may not be your choice. Or Child Protective Services may step in.

Who will make healthcare decisions for you if you are unable to do so for yourself?

If you want a say in your medical treatments should you become terminally ill or incapacitated, you need one or more of the following: a *living will*, an *advance healthcare directive*, or a *healthcare proxy*. These allow you to specify, for example, whether you want to be put on life support (or not), and under what circumstances. They also let you name someone to make medical decisions on your behalf if you are unable to do so yourself.

Who will make financial and business decisions for you if you are ill or disabled?

A *power of attorney* (POA) lets you name someone to act on your behalf in financial or business matters.

Who gets your stuff?

There are three areas to pay attention to when planning how to bequeath your stuff: titling, beneficiaries, and your will.

- *Titling* is about who officially owns your assets. This can be you alone, you with others, or some legal entity (such as a trust which you control). If you own something jointly with another person, particularly a spouse, it is often as joint tenants with rights of survivorship, meaning the other person ends up with the entire thing if you die first. In that case, even if you do have a will, it won't enter the picture. (There are other ways to own things jointly, with different rules in different states.)

- If you name *beneficiaries* on specific assets, such as retirement accounts and life insurance, they get the payout when you die. Normally, if you designate someone as a beneficiary, they inherit it regardless of what your will says. Stay on top of this! If you divorce and still have your ex as a beneficiary, they may inherit an account even if you have left everything to someone else in your will (though some states and plans automatically revoke spouses as beneficiaries after a divorce.) Or if you specifically name your first child as a beneficiary and don't update the designation when you have your second (or third, or sixth), your first child could end up with everything.
- A *Last Will and Testament* lets you decide who to leave your stuff to. If you don't have one, the *intestate* laws of your state will lay out how things are to be split among your heirs. That may not be as you like it. You might think your will is your private business, but after you die it becomes public, along with a list of everything it passes on. It goes through a court process known as *probate*. In some states this is time-consuming and expensive. Many people, once they've accumulated some assets, like to set up what's known as a "living trust" to avoid the probate process and keep their affairs private.

Who will settle your affairs in the event of your demise?

In a will you select an *executor* to wrap up your affairs. This should be someone you trust to be competent and follow your wishes. Often it makes sense to pick a family member or friend; but it can also be a professional, e.g., a lawyer, who will do it for a fee. If you don't appoint an executor, a court will appoint one for you.

Putting a Plan in Place

Estate planning is mostly governed by state laws. Make sure you get guidance specific to your state. Where do you turn? A competent attorney who will draft your documents is the best way to go. You'll have an initial meeting, receive a draft for review, and then return to sign the documents with witnesses present. Fees can vary but expect to pay $300 to $1,200 or more.[55]

Alternatively, you can write your own will. Consider using an online program, such as **Legalzoom.com**, or **Willmaker** software, to create documents at home. Once you have the documents make sure you sign them, with witnesses and notaries as required by your state.

---

[55] Mary Randolph, "How Much Will a Lawyer Charge to Write Your Will?", Nolo.com, accessed 3/28/2020

Chapter 20: Potential Money

Elle Woods: "I don't need back-ups. I'm going to Harvard."

CULA Advisor: "Well then, you'll need excellent recommendations from your professors."

Elle Woods: "Okay."

CULA Advisor: "And a heck of an admissions essay."

Elle Woods: "Right."

CULA Advisor: "And at least a 175 on your LSATs."

Elle Woods: "I once had to judge a tighty-whitey contest for Lambda Kappa Pi. Trust me, I can handle anything."

– Legally Blonde (2001)

One of the great things about our human capital is that though it is finite, it is not fixed. We can invest in it to enhance our earnings potential (as well as our general well-being). Up to a point. Two of the best investments we can make are *health* and *education*.

Health

Investing in health—leading a healthy lifestyle—allows us to work longer if we choose to or need to, with lower medical expenses and greater productivity. Of course, that is true *on average*, not a guarantee for any one of us. While recommendations seem to change all the time, here is one list of factors that in a large study contributed to a significantly longer lifespan:[56]

- *Diet*: Favor vegetables, fruits, nuts, whole grains, healthy fats, and omega-3 fatty acids. Avoid red and processed meats, sugar-sweetened beverages, trans fat, and sodium.
- *Exercise*: Thirty minutes of moderate to vigorous activity per day.
- *Weight*: Maintain a body mass index (BMI) of 18.5 to 24.9.
- *Smoking*: Don't.
- *Alcohol*: No more than one drink per day for women or two for men.

Now you have another reason to take care of your health: look at it as a financial investment.

Education

Education is the other big investment you can make in your earnings potential. High school graduates on average earn more than those who don't graduate. College graduates earn more than high school graduates. Unfortunately, it's not always just about learning: research suggests that a good part of the bang for your education buck comes from *actually graduating*. Getting the degree matters. This is known as the "sheepskin effect." Three years of college don't get you three quarters of the earnings benefit of a four-year degree.

This all sounds nice in theory, but remember: you are not the average. To repeat what I said about student loans in Chapter 8: Whether college makes financial sense depends on the degree you pursue. It depends on your age, the income you can expect after graduation, and the earnings you give up while in school.

---

[56] Monique Tellow, "Healthy Lifestyle: 5 Keys to a Longer Life," Harvard Health Blog, 3/25/2020

A traditional college education comes with a big price tag, to say nothing of post-graduate training such as law school or medical school. So as with any big investment, it's important to remain flexible and check out different options. One of the obvious ways to lower the burden is to consider state colleges with their lower in-state tuition costs.

Then there are grants and scholarships for which you can apply. This can involve some work but can yield thousands of dollars in support.

Unsure about heading off to a four-year program? Consider a two-year community college degree. With good grades, if you decide to continue your college education, transferring to a four-year state school is quite feasible. You can also save a significant chunk because community colleges cost much less compared with spending those first two years at a four-year school.

Tread cautiously with "for profit" colleges. While not uniformly bad, they tend to have low graduation rates and leave students with more debt than not-for-profit schools.[57] Many students have found themselves pushed into expensive loans, and in multiple cases the schools have gone out of business and left students with a pile of debt and no degree.

If you are a stellar student and your family is poor, education can be a breakout opportunity. Going to an elite college may not even be on your radar screen. Don't dismiss the idea. Many leading private colleges will evaluate your application without considering your finances. (They are "need blind.") Of those, many provide financial aid packages to meet your full demonstrated financial need. And a subset, including most of the Ivy League schools, promise to do so with grants and scholarships, meaning you can graduate without massive student debt.

---

[57] Center for Responsible Lending, "The State of For-Profit Colleges," 1/29/2019

At the end of the day, education doesn't begin or end with a degree: it's an ongoing process. You gain human capital by accumulating experience, establishing a professional network, and acquiring skills. Some fields, such as computer programming, are more open than others to people without formal degrees if you can demonstrate competence. Others may require specific certifications or exams. After that you learn on the job, from colleagues, or by pursuing additional training. Lots of skills can be learned at very low cost online and require mostly time and commitment.

As the term suggests: you build *human capital* through *human effort*.

Resources

Government and Regulatory Agencies		
College Scorecard	Detailed U.S. Department of Education info on cost of study, loans, and income by school and major	**https://collegescorecard.ed.gov/**

Businesses		
Finaid.org	Resource to find scholarships (and info on saving for college and borrowing)	**https://www.finaid.org/scholarships/**

Chapter 21: Protecting Future Money

Walter Neff: "Who'd you think I was anyway? The guy that walks into a good-looking dame's front parlor and says, 'Good afternoon, I sell accident insurance on husbands... you got one that's been around too long? One you'd like to turn into a little hard cash?'"

– Double Indemnity (1944)

One of the not-so-great things is that our human capital is not guaranteed. Life can go off the rails and keep us from working in our chosen profession, or at all.

To provide at least some hard cash when life turns dire, you need... stay with me here... insurance.

Protecting Your Income

The most important is *disability insurance*. As the name implies, this insurance pays if you cannot work due to a disability. The top three causes of long-term disability are cancer, injury, and back disorders.[58] These and many others can sideline anyone at any time.

In almost every state, employers are required to provide *workers compensation insurance*. Workers compensation pays you a benefit if you become injured or disabled *at work*. Employers pay the premiums for this insurance.

---

[58] Unum.com, "Top Causes of Disability", 5/3/2019, accessed 10/22/2019

Work-related injuries only account for a small percentage of disabilities. What if you become disabled *outside of work*?

If you have worked at least five years and you become disabled you may be eligible to receive money from the federal government (*Social Security Disability Insurance*), but it's not a lot, and if you can do *any* job, you'll have to take it. Social Security Disability is a safety net, but it is a challenge to make ends meet with it.

Many larger employers offer short-term and long-term disability insurance as part of their benefit packages. This is valuable. But remember that if you leave the employer you may no longer be covered.

If you are self-employed or don't have coverage through your employer, consider buying private disability insurance, especially if you have made significant investments in your profession or have a lot of debt.

Protecting Your Loved Ones

If family or others depend on your income consider buying *life insurance*. Life insurance pays money to a *beneficiary* if you die. Many larger employers provide up to $50,000 of insurance for free. They may also let you pay an extra premium out of your paycheck for a higher benefit. This type of "group" policy has some drawbacks. The premiums often increase every few years. Also, you may not be able get the amount of insurance you need and if you switch employers, you may not be able to take it with you. If you are healthy, it often makes sense to buy "individual" life insurance instead of, or on top of, group insurance.

Life Insurance You Need

The only kind you should buy is *term insurance*, specifically *level* term insurance. You pay a fixed premium every year for a set period, usually between ten and thirty years. If you die during this period, your beneficiary receives the death benefit. If you don't, the benefit is that you got to live.

Term insurance is a simple product. The market is competitive, and you can readily get quotes online. For example, a thirty-year policy with a $1,000,000 benefit from a high-quality insurance company would cost a healthy thirty-year-old woman about $500 a year.[59] Rates for men are a bit higher because they don't live as long. When you apply to buy a policy the insurance company will *underwrite* your application, meaning they will estimate the risk of you dying earlier than average. If you smoke, have known health risks, or engage in dangerous activities, you have to tell them and may have to pay higher premiums. For larger policies, the insurance company may do a basic medical exam.

How much life insurance should you buy? It depends on your situation. How dependent are your beneficiaries on your income? How much can they replace from other sources? Do they have to continue to pay down debt, such as a mortgage? Also think about how long you will need insurance. If it's to support your children, you probably don't need it when they are grown, you're retired, and your mortgage is paid off. Buying for shorter terms reduces the premiums.

There are a number of online calculators (such as the one from **Life Happens**) to help you figure out how much insurance you need. Your beneficiaries won't have to pay income tax on life insurance benefits they receive, so the full amount will be available to cover expenses.

Life Insurance You Don't Need

Insurance agents may try to convince you to buy other types of life insurance, such as *whole life*, *universal life*, *indexed universal life*, or *variable universal life*. With each of these, you pay extra money (many times the term life premium) that the insurance company invests on

---

59 Quote for a thirty-year-old healthy female non-smoker retrieved from Term4Sale.com on 3/28/2020

your behalf. You can do better investing on your own. Agents want to sell these policies because the commissions are far larger than for selling a term life policy. You may get flimflam about "permanent" insurance and "tax benefits" in the sales pitch. Don't take the bait. If your agent gets too pushy, find another agent.

Where to Get It

It's important to buy your policy from a company that is likely to be around. Look for ratings of AA/Aa2 or better from Standard and Poor's and Moody's; though if the premium is a lot lower a company with a rating of A+ or better from A.M. Best is also okay. Here are some of the strongest companies.

Company	S&P/Moody's	A.M. Best	Term Life	Disability Income
Northwestern Mutual	AA+/Aaa	A++	X	X
New York Life	AA+/Aaa	A++	X	
Guardian	AA+/Aa2	A++	X	X
MassMutual	AA+/Aa3	A++	X	X
State Farm	AA/--	A++	X	X
Legal & General (Banner Life)	AA/--	A+	X	
Prudential	AA-/Aa3	A+	X	

Source: Company websites accessed 3/29/2020

As with annuities, you buy disability and life insurance from an insurance agent. Agents are either *independent*, representing a variety of companies, or *captive* with a single company. By law, for a given insurance policy, you pay the same premium to the insurance company regardless of who sells it to you. "Lowest price" guarantees are meaningless.

A good agent can help you compare policies from different companies and help you through the underwriting process if your health is not stellar. But be aware that agents have an incentive to 1) sell you insurance you don't need and 2) steer you to companies they represent that pay them the highest commissions or bonuses.

You can check out quotes online. For term life, **Policygenius** is an online independent agency representing a broad selection of companies. **Term4sale** will give you quotes and suggest life insurance agents in your area. **Haven Life** offers policies from MassMutual.

For disability insurance, the largest insurers have their own captive agents—check out their websites. **Life Happens** has an agent locator. Also ask around for references that can help locate someone trustworthy with experience in your profession.

Resources

Government and Regulatory Agencies		
USA.gov Benefits and Insurance for People with Disabilities	Government information on Social Security disability benefits and related topics	**https://www.usa.gov/disability-benefits-insurance**
U.S. Department of Labor	Directory of state workers compensation offices	**https://www.dol.gov/owcp/dfec/**
DOL Office of Workers Compensation Programs	Information on federal workers compensation programs	**https://www.dol.gov/owcp/**

Businesses		
Life Happens	Industry group founded by agents. Information and calculators	**https://lifehappens.org/**

Chapter 22: Protecting Saved Money

Billy Ray Valentine: "That was a cheap vase, right? That was a fake? Right?"

Randolph Duke: "I believe we paid $35,000. But if I remember correctly, we valued it for the insurance company at $50,000. You see, Mortimer? William has already made us $15,000."

– Trading Places (1983)

Disability insurance and life insurance protect your human capital and replace your income if something bad happens to you. But what about your hard-earned net worth? Natural disasters, accidents, theft, lawsuits...all have the potential to put a big dent in your savings, even wipe them out entirely. To protect against this, you need *property and casualty insurance*.

Broadly speaking, property insurance pays you if your property—home, car, boat, etc.—is damaged or stolen. Casualty insurance pays if you are found to be at fault (liable) for causing damage to others via your home, car, boat, etc. Most policies combine the two. The most common types of property and casualty insurance for individuals are automobile insurance, renters insurance, and homeowners insurance.

It's useful to think for a moment about how insurance companies make money. They collect premiums from many thousands of customers and sometime later pay claims to a few. The goal is to collect more than is paid out. In the meantime, they get to invest the premiums. As Warren Buffett, the fabled chief of one of the largest insurance companies, put it, "This combination allows us to enjoy the use of free money—and, better yet, get paid for holding it."[60]

Right away, you can see that insurance companies have a strong incentive not to pay claims. One way they do this is to limit what is covered from the get-go. So-called *named peril* policies have a list of the kinds of losses that will be covered. For things not on the list, you're on your own. *Open peril* policies pay for any loss but list certain *exclusions*. For example, one of the major exclusions in most homeowner insurance policies is damage caused by floods.

Automobile Insurance

I am sure you are an above-average driver. We all are. So we can relate to the situation where "The guy was all over the road; I had to swerve a number of times before I hit him."[61] It's because that guy is on the road that we need to get auto insurance.

There are several kinds of insurance coverage that come bundled in a policy. Depending on where you live, some are mandatory:

	Paid to	**Whose Fault?**	**For What?**
Liability	Others	Yours	Injury to others or property damage
"No fault"	You	Yours or others'	Injury to you or your passengers
Uninsured motorist	You	Others'	Injury or property damage to you or your passengers
Collision	You	Yours	Damage to your car
Comprehensive	You	Others'	Theft or other type of damage to your car

[60] Berkshire Hathaway, "Letter to Shareholders", February 26, 2010, p. 6

[61] The Old Farmer's Almanac, "Funny Car Accident Reports and More Humor", 6/30/2017

Let's go through them.

Almost all states require you to have *some* automobile liability insurance. A typical state requirement is that you have insurance that pays up to $25,000 to each person injured, up to $50,000 for any one accident involving multiple people, and up to $10,000 to pay for property damage. If the actual costs are higher than these *policy limits*, you owe the difference. Unfortunately, these minimums are not nearly enough if somebody is seriously injured. You should buy $300,000 of liability insurance or more.

Some states also require you to have no-fault insurance. No-fault insurance cuts through the "he-said, she-said." It pays you if you're injured regardless of who was at fault in an accident.

Another requirement in some states is uninsured motorist coverage. Since insurance is expensive, you may end up in an accident with someone who does not have any, or maybe has just the bare minimum. Even if they legally owe you, they simply may not have the money. That's when uninsured motorist coverage steps in and pays your expenses.

On the other hand, nobody *requires* you to buy comprehensive or collision insurance because nobody cares if your car is stolen or you crack it up with your above-average driving. You need to decide whether this coverage is worth the cost. If you have a cheap old car because you are saving like mad it might make sense to just skip it.

How to Have Low Premiums

Auto insurance isn't cheap. The cost depends a lot on where you live, your age, gender, marital status, driving record, credit history...even your grades if you are still in school. The major things you can do to lower the cost of auto insurance are:

- Own a cheap car
- Maintain a clean driving record
- Buy less insurance (but don't skimp on liability coverage)
- Shop around to get multiple quotes (and repeat every few years)

- Increase your deductibles (the amount you pay out of pocket before the insurance kicks in)
- Qualify for safe-driver, good-student, and other discounts offered by the insurer
- Maintain a good credit score
- Get renters or homeowners insurance from the same insurance company to get a discount

You can also get discounts based on how you drive (so-called *usage-based* insurance). By letting the insurance company track your driving, through a device installed in your car or through your smartphone, you may be able to pay less. If you only drive occasionally, you can even buy insurance by the mile.

Where to Get It

You want an auto insurance company that has low premiums and doesn't give you hard time if you need a claim paid. You can readily get quotes from most large insurers by going to their websites or calling an agent. The five largest are: *State Farm*, *Geico*, *Progressive*, *Allstate*, and *USAA*, but there are many others. Make sure to compare costs for similar coverage. You can compare quotes online through the agencies listed at the end of the chapter. You can also go to an independent insurance agent in your area to see if there are good deals to be had among lesser-known but reputable insurance companies.

The larger insurers all offer usage-based insurance discounts. There are some techy new companies that are taking the concept to the next level. **Root Insurance** weeds out the riskiest drivers and passes the savings on to those drivers it agrees to insure. **Metromile** charges a low monthly premium and an additional per-mile charge.

How to Get a Claim Paid

If you are in an accident, even a minor one, call 911. The police will try to ascertain who is at fault and fill out an accident report. This is your best ammunition in a claim and may even be required by the insurance company. Stay calm and objective. Don't get sucked into arguments. Don't admit guilt. If possible, get information on the other driver(s) by taking a picture of their license and verifying their address and phone number. If there are witnesses, try to get their names and phone numbers. Take pictures of the accident scene and any damage. Wait until things (and you) are settled down before you contact your insurance company. If the accident is your fault and pretty minor it may not make sense to file a claim. You may be better off paying a few hundred dollars out of your own pocket to avoid an increase in your insurance premiums.

Renters and Homeowners Insurance

Renters Insurance

If you rent your home and have a bunch of stuff in it, you should probably get renters insurance. Many landlords require it. If your stuff is lost in a fire, stolen, or otherwise damaged, renters insurance will pay for repairing or replacing it. Renters insurance is usually named peril insurance; if something happens for a reason that is not on the list it won't be covered. Also, some of your belongings may not be covered—you need to tell the insurance company about fancy jewelry, expensive collectibles, and the like. They may agree to add these for an additional charge.

How much do you get if you file a claim? Basic renters insurance will pay you whatever your stuff is worth when it's lost or damaged. This is known as the *actual cash value*. Think of it this way: A ten-year-old couch is worth a lot less than one you just bought a month ago, so you'll get a lot less for it. With actual cash value you could use the insurance money to buy another ten-year old couch at a garage sale. But that may not be so appealing. Instead, you can opt for *replacement cost* coverage. This means that the insurance company will pay you what it would cost to buy a comparable—but new—couch today.

Renters insurance also includes liability coverage in case somebody gets hurt at your place or you are responsible for damage to others' property.

Homeowners Insurance

If you own a home, you should get homeowners insurance. It's required by lenders if you have a mortgage, but important protection even if you don't. Homeowners insurance will pay to repair or rebuild your house if it's damaged. Like renters insurance, it also covers your belongings and includes liability coverage in the event someone gets hurt on your property (for example, if your dog bites the neighbor or a delivery guy slips on your front steps).

Homeowners insurance can be either named peril or open peril coverage with exclusions. Understand what is and is not covered by your policy.

Homeowners insurance usually pays at least replacement cost, up to the policy limit you've insured the home for. But it's possible for the cost of rebuilding to be higher. For example, local labor and materials often become more expensive after a natural disaster. To make sure that the full cost of rebuilding is covered even beyond the policy limit you can pay extra and opt for *guaranteed replacement cost* coverage.

How to Have Low Premiums

As with auto insurance, it's smart to get some bids every few years. Insurance companies adjust the estimated cost to rebuild or repair your home every year. You don't want to be over-insured, paying more premium than necessary. You also don't want to be under-insured and find out that insurance will only cover a fraction of any loss.

Another way to reduce your premium is to install a centrally monitored fire and burglar alarm. And, as with all types of insurance, if you increase your deductible, you will pay lower premiums.

Where to Get It

Some of the big insurance companies that sell automobile insurance also sell renters and homeowners insurance. Again, the best way is to compare what's covered and get several quotes. As with automobile insurance, a good independent agent can help, or check out quotes from the online agencies listed at the end of the chapter. Some newer tech-driven insurance companies that are hungry for business might give you a good deal. Depending on where you live, check out **Lemonade**. While originally focused on auto insurance, **Root Insurance** now also offers renters and homeowners insurance in some state.

Umbrella Insurance

As your net worth (hopefully) grows, the liability insurance included with auto and homeowners policies may not be enough. The more wealth you accumulate, the fatter a target you are for a lawsuit. To protect against this you should buy *umbrella insurance*, which is extra liability insurance that pays out if your other insurance is used up. Umbrella insurance is relatively cheap because it is unlikely that you will use it, but it protects you against rare, large events. Usually it's a separate policy that insurance companies will only sell you if you have auto or homeowners insurance with them. How much umbrella insurance do you need? As a rule of thumb make sure your auto liability and umbrella coverage are at least equal to your net worth.

Got Insurance? Don't File a Claim

Insurers don't like claims. Don't submit one unless it's big and you have to. Companies are apt to increase your premium and may even drop you entirely if you are costing them too much or are too quick to file claims. Switching to another insurer may not help. Any claim you initiate, whether you get paid or not, and sometimes even if you just *inquire* about making a claim, is reported to the Comprehensive Loss Underwriting Exchange (CLUE). Insurers check your CLUE report when deciding whether to insure you and how much to charge. Claims stay on your CLUE report for seven years. You're entitled to receive a free copy of your report. Contact **LexisNexis®** to get one.

Resources

Government and Regulatory Agencies		
National Association of Insurance Commissioners (NAIC)	Consumer page from the umbrella organization of state insurance regulators. Get guides on insurance and complaint statistics on insurance companies	**https://content.naic.org/consumer.htm**
Businesses		
LexisNexis® Risk Solutions	Consumer reporting company. Compiles risk reports on consumers. Check the report on you for free once a year	**https://consumer.risk.lexisnexis.com/**
Compare.com Coverhound Insurify Policygenius The Zebra	Online insurance agencies providing quotes for auto, homeowner, renters, and other property and casualty insurance	**https://www.compare.com/** **https://coverhound.com/** **https://insurify.com/** **https://www.policygenius.com/** **https://www.thezebra.com/**

Chapter 23: Money and Health

Woody Grant: "I won a million dollars."

ER Doctor: "Congratulations. That'll just about pay for a day in the hospital."

– Nebraska (2013)

It's advisable, though not always affordable, to have health insurance. Most Americans get theirs in one of four ways:

- Through an employer
- On their own in the "individual" market
- Through Medicaid if they are disabled or have low incomes
- Through Medicare if they are sixty-five or older or disabled

Also, close to nine million people in the U.S. get insurance from the Department of Veterans Affairs (VA).

The cost of insurance, what is covered, and which insurance can be used to pay for which treatments vary widely. It's also really hard to find out in advance what medical care will cost and how much will be covered by insurance. Prepare to be surprised. Unpleasantly.

Health insurance (except Medicaid in many states) generally does not pay for contact lenses and glasses, dental care, and hearing aids. The same goes for *long-term care*, such as extended nursing home stays. These all require separate insurance.

Health Insurance Lingo

Let's get some terminology out of the way.

Deductible: A dollar amount that you have to pay before the insurance company pays anything. For health insurance, deductibles are *yearly* amounts.

Co-payment: A fixed dollar amount you're expected to pay—for example, $20 per doctor visit.

Co-insurance: A percentage of the cost of a procedure or drug that you are expected to pay after you've reached the deductible.

Out-of-pocket maximum: The most you have to pay in a year for procedures that are covered by the insurance plan. Co-insurance stops at this amount; the insurance company pays 100 percent of additional charges.

Network: A group of hospitals, doctors, pharmacies, and other providers with which the insurance company has negotiated rates for different procedures. Insurance companies will cover more costs when you use "in-network" providers than "out-of-network" providers.

Health Maintenance Organizations (HMOs): Insurance organizations that *require* you to use "in-network" providers. Out-of-network providers are on your own dime.

Preferred Provider Organizations (PPOs): Plans where your cost is lower if you use an in-network provider but there is some coverage for out-of-network costs.

High-Deductible Health Plan (HDHP): A policy which meets various requirements that will allow you invest in a Health Savings Account (HSA). As the name suggests, the main feature is that the deductible is high: in 2020 at least $1,400 for an individual or $2,800 for a family.

Coverage at Work

Many employees receive health insurance at work. Unfortunately, there is no "one size," so it's important to review the plans that are available to you. Key questions to ask are:

- Is coverage also available for my spouse/partner and children? Compare costs if your spouse/partner also has insurance at work.
- Are there *exclusions* that affect me (e.g., pre-existing conditions, mental health services, etc.)?
- What are the deductibles, co-pays, maximums, etc., compared with my expected expenses?
- Do I have doctors or hospitals that I prefer to visit and, if so, are they in the plan network?
- What does the insurance cost? Recognize that what is taken out of your paycheck is often only a fraction of the cost. Your employer picks up the rest (though you can be sure that your salary is lower as a result). A total yearly cost of $20,000 for a family plan is not unusual. Your employer's share of the premium is shown on your year-end W-2.
- Do I need a referral from a primary care doctor to see specialists?
- Do I need pre-approval from the insurance company for elective procedures?
- If I choose an HDHP does my employer contribute to an HSA for me?

Remember, you can usually change plans once a year. If you are healthy and don't anticipate any significant expense, a high-deductible plan and HSA may make sense; if you expect higher expenses, a more expensive plan with more generous benefits might be better.

If you leave your job, you can choose to continue your employer health coverage for up to eighteen months under what is known as COBRA coverage.[62] The catch: You pay the full cost of coverage.

Individual Coverage

If you don't have insurance at work or through a parent or partner's plan you need to look to the individual insurance market. "Individual" just means you're not part of a larger group; you can still get a policy to cover your entire household.

Brace yourself for sticker shock and a cumbersome sign-up process. Start by looking at the "Marketplace" (**www.healthcare.gov**) created by Affordable Care Act ("ACA", also known as "Obamacare") to see how to enroll in your state. There is an annual enrollment period that runs for a few weeks starting in November of each year, though you can also sign up if you have a life change such as losing other insurance, getting married, or having a child.

If your income isn't too high, the government pays part or even all of your premium for policies bought through the Marketplace. How much depends on your income relative to the national poverty level. You get this subsidy by telling the government how much you *expect* to make in the coming year. Later, when you file taxes on your *actual* income, you settle up by paying more or less in income taxes for the year.

---

[62] In certain circumstances you may be eligible for 36 months of COBRA coverage. "COBRA" stands for "Consolidated Omnibus Budget Reconciliation Act"...you had to ask, didn't you?

National Poverty Level (Annual Income) in 2020[63]

Size of Household	Lower 48	Alaska	Hawaii
1	$12,760	$15,950	$14,680
2	$17,240	$21,550	$19,830
3	$21,720	$27,150	$24,980
4	$26,200	$32,750	$30,130
5	$30,680	$38,350	$35,280
6	$35,160	$43,950	$40,430

You can also buy an individual policy that is not sold through the Marketplace. This may give you more choices but be aware that these policies don't always cover everything Marketplace policies must cover, and they are not eligible for the government subsidies.

Medicaid

Medicaid and the related Children's Health Insurance Program (CHIP) provide basic health coverage for about 72.5 million Americans—more than one out of five. Eligibility varies by state; thirty-seven have "expanded" Medicaid to cover households earning up to about a third more than the national poverty level. The rules are complex; to find out more start by getting info on your home state's program.

Medicare

When you turn sixty-five you should enroll in Medicare. One misconception is that Medicare is free. It's not. You pay premiums and if you don't enroll on time, you'll face life-long higher costs.[64]

---

[63] Department of Health and Human Services, https://aspe.hhs.gov/poverty-guidelines, accessed 3/31/2020

[64] You can delay enrolling if you're still working and have insurance through work. But make sure your insurance is "eligible"

Medicare comes in several "parts":

Part A covers hospital stays. It's free if you've paid FICA taxes for at least ten years. Otherwise, your pay a premium (in 2020, up to $458 a month).

Part B covers doctor visits and other "outpatient" services. You pay a premium for Part B coverage which is often taken out of your Social Security check. The basic premium in 2020 was $145 a month for Part B, more if you made more than $87,000 ($174,000 as a couple). There is also an annual deductible for Part B, $198 in 2020.

Part C and *Part D* are extra policies that you can buy from insurance companies. Part C (known as *Medicare Advantage*) plans roll all your Medicare (Parts A, B, and usually D) into one package. The policies provide more coverage but are HMOs or PPOs that either don't cover out-of-network costs at all or only at a lower rate.

Part D policies are specifically for prescription drugs. Most Medicare Advantage policies include prescription drugs, so you wouldn't get a Part D policy if you opt for a Medicare Advantage policy.

Finally, *Medigap* (or Medicare Supplement) policies are policies you can buy to "fill the gaps" in Medicare coverage. They cover deductibles and coinsurance among other things. You wouldn't get a Medigap policy if you opt for a Medicare Advantage plan.

It's all a lot more complicated than it needs to be, but that's what it is. If you're nearing sixty-five take some time to figure it out.

When Insurance Doesn't Pay

Stuck with a massive medical bill? Welcome to America's healthcare system, which serves up a steady diet of denied claims, unaffordable insurance, outrageous charges, "surprise" bills, and hospitals suing patients for non-payment. There's no single or easy way to navigate this mess, but here are some tips from insiders:[65]

Before Getting Care

Figure out whether it's medically necessary. Don't just go with the first recommendation. Sometimes procedures are recommended "just in case" or because doctors want to avoid being sued. Or they become an accepted practice even though there is little evidence of any benefit; an example is the overuse of arterial stents.[66]

Comparison shop. If it's not an emergency, call around to different hospitals and providers and try to find out what a procedure will cost you out-of-pocket. Prices vary dramatically, often with little difference in quality. Be persistent because getting the information can be tough. You can also research prices on-line for different procedures in your area.

Once you have a sense for what a procedure should cost, negotiate. Offer to pay cash in advance as opposed to going through insurance (especially if you want to use an out-of-network provider or won't reach your deductible). Some providers will give you a deal to avoid the hassle of dealing with insurance companies. Taking this concept to the next level, you can even go outside the country and get common procedures for much less (known as "medical tourism").

Learn about the active ingredients in medications and look for generic substitutes. Many brand-name drugs are nearly identical to medicines that are older and available in generic form.

---

[65] This section draws from two authors; both are MDs and have done extensive research and reporting on these issues. See Rosenthal, Elisabeth, *An American Sickness: How Healthcare Became Big Business and How You Can Take It Back*, Penguin Books, New York, 2017; and Makary, Marty, *The Price We Pay: What Broke American Healthcare –And How to Fix It*, Bloomsbury Publishing, New York, 2019

[66] Harvard Health Publishing, "When Do You Need a Heart Stent?", 10/13/2020

During Care

When you are at the doctor, let alone in the ER, you feel lousy and vulnerable. You're in no mood to haggle. But ideally you should ask questions to understand which tests and procedures are going to be run and why you need them. "Oh, it's standard practice" is not a good answer.

If you're told you will be kept in the hospital make sure you're *admitted* (covered by insurance), not just kept for *observation* (not covered by insurance). Ask for a semi-private room rather than a private room (more expensive). Insist on in-network providers only (write it on hospital admission papers).

Afterwards

If you receive a medical bill, do not just pay it. Request itemization of charges and get explanations for anything you don't understand. Bills are rife with errors. Try to inform yourself about typical costs and immediately challenge and negotiate outsized charges. Check if your employer has a *patient advocate*; consider hiring one for especially large bills. If your insurance claim is denied, understand why and your right to appeal.

Resources

Government and Regulatory Agencies		
Healthcare.gov	Gateway to getting Obamacare coverage in each state	**healthcare.gov**
Medicaid.gov	Links to Medicaid offices in each state	**https://www.medicaid.gov/state-overviews/index.html**
Medicare.gov	All things Medicare. It's a pretty good site. And it's official.	**medicare.gov**
SHIPs	State Health Insurance Assistance Programs is a network of volunteer counselors to give advice on Medicare issues	**shiptacare.org**

Businesses		
Kaiser Family Foundation	Non-profit research organization with extensive data on healthcare. Map with current status of Medicaid in each state	**https://www.kff.org/medicaid/**
AARP	Non-profit membership organization that lobbies on issues affecting old people and sells insurance and other services	**https://www.aarp.org/health/medicare-insurance/**
Fair Health	Non-profit that collects data and provides estimates of healthcare prices	**https://www.fairhealthconsumer.org/**
New Choice Health	Commercial site with health care price data comparisons	**https://www.newchoicehealth.com/**
Turquoise Health	Startup company aggregating price data from providers across the country	**https://turquoise.health/**
GoodRX	Company that negotiates discounted drug prices for consumers at local pharmacies	**goodrx.com**

Chapter 24: Money Scams

Doyle Lonnegan: "Your boss is quite a card player, Mr. Kelly. How does he do it?"

Johnny Hooker: "He cheats."

– The Sting (1973)

When you have money, there's always someone wanting to separate you from it. The "legal" method is to make you pay too much for stuff you don't need. Then there are the scam artists and fraudsters. It can be a fine line.

The Weakest Link

It's you. Don't think you can't be conned, scammed, phished, or tricked. Just ask former clients of **Bernie Madoff**. Ask the two ex-secretaries of state who sat on the board of directors of **Theranos**. Ask former CIA Director **John Brennan** or Amazon chairman **Jeff Bezos**. All have been victims.

Accept that everyone is vulnerable and be suspicious. Scams rely on *trust*: they can pretend to come from government organizations, charities, friends, and family. Understand the IRS won't call you out of the blue. Your bank won't ask for your password over the phone. Those Billie Eilish tickets may be duds.

Scams ebb and flow with current events and the seasons. Census scams were in vogue in 2020. Unemployment scams were big business during the pandemic. Try to keep up to date with the what's hot. You can sign up for consumer alerts from the **Federal Trade Commission**.

To protect yourself, get names and call-back numbers from anyone asking for information over the phone. Don't click on email attachments or hyperlinks, even if they came from your mother, unless you are confident that they are legitimate. Don't wire money to people you don't know. Don't deposit unknown checks you receive in the mail.

When it comes to investing, remember that a high return comes with more risk. The old adage applies: If it sounds too good to be true, it probably is. People—well-intentioned or otherwise—will pitch all sorts of investment schemes that supposedly will make you money with virtually no risk. Turn the tables and ask how you can *lose* money. If you don't get a clear answer, or if the answer doesn't make sense, stay away.

Phishing, Vishing, Smishing

Phishing happens through social media, email, voice calls, and messages. Here are tips from the Cybersecurity and Infrastructure Security Agency (CISA) on how to keep alert to phishing attempts:[67]

- Watch for sender's addresses that resemble reputable companies or organizations.
- Beware of generic greetings such as "Dear Customer."
- Hover over links to inspect the URLs that they link to.
- Watch for wierd, bad, or inappropriate spelling & grammer.
- Don't download unknown attachments.

We've all heard these. Still, we fall prey.

---

[67] Cybersecurity and Infrastructure Security Agency, "Security Tip (ST04-014) Avoiding Social Engineering and Phishing Attacks", 8/25/2020

Cybersecurity

Much of your financial life is on-line. This is great for cost, speed, and choice. It also makes you a target. You need to protect yourself. Security specialist Joel de la Garza has a concise to-do list.[68]

Passwords

You don't use "password", "qwerty", "sunshine", "iloveyou", or "123456", do you?[69] And you don't use personal information such as your name, address, birthdate, pet's name, or phone number in your passwords, right? Right.

So how do you choose a good password?

Make it long. A computer can figure short ones out by "brute force," i.e., running through all the possibilities. It will take just as long to figure out "password" as it will "A$kzzPR#"—just a few minutes with enough computing power. Use long word strings with upper- and lower-case letters, numbers, and special characters ("plumber$Dividing6#Botox" anyone?) But avoid common phrases, song lyrics, or quotes.

Don't reuse it. Have a different password for every account. If somebody gets into one, they won't have access to others.

Change it regularly. Especially if you've been subject to a data breach, which most people have.

Don't write it down. Generate passwords and save them in a secure password manager such as **Dashlane** or **Keeper**.[70]

---

[68] Joel de la Garza, "16 Steps to Securing Your Data (and Life)", blogpost at Andreesen Horowitz, November 12, 2019

[69] Wikipedia.com, "List of the Most Common Passwords", accessed 4/14/2020

[70] Neil J. Rubenking and Ben Moore, "The Best Password Managers for 2021", PCmag.com, updated 2/ 17/ 2021, accessed 3/23/2021

Two-Factor Authentication (2FA)

Enable two-factor authentication in any account that offers it, including all your bank and brokerage accounts and your email accounts. With 2FA you receive a unique code each time you log in. This may be sent to you by text message, phone call, email, through an authentication app, or a physical security key.

Even 2FA is not a sure thing. As a further level of security be sure to enable enhanced security options with your cellphone carrier, if they offer it.

Networks

Don't use "open" networks (coffee shops, hotels, airports, etc.) or WiFi "hotspots" for anything confidential. Instead use your phone's cellular data or set up a Virtual Private Network (VPN).

Don't use public or shared computers. If it's unavoidable, make sure to log out of your accounts, clear the cookies and other information in the browser settings, and close the program.

Identity Theft

Chances are good that your personal information is already for sale on the dark web. It may just be a matter of time before someone tries to use your identity for profit. During the COVID-19 pandemic, a widespread fraud was the use of stolen personal information to apply for unemployment payments. So what can you do to protect yourself?

The basic steps are outlined by the Federal Trade Commission at **https://identitytheft.gov/**. Even before you are actively combating an event, take the cybersecurity steps outlined above to prevent unauthorized access to your financial accounts.

Also put in place credit freezes at each of the three major credit bureaus (see Chapter 9) and at Chexsystems (see Chapter 4).

Resources

Government and Regulatory Agencies		
USA.gov	Examples of common scams and how to protect yourself	**https://www.usa.gov/common-scams-frauds#item-212864**
Cybersecurity and Infrastructure Security Agency (CISA)	Social engineering and phishing info	**https://www.us-cert.gov/ncas/tips/ST04-014**
	Password tips and more	**https://www.us-cert.gov/ncas/tips/ST04-002**
Federal Trade Commission	How to respond to identity theft	**https://identitytheft.gov/**

Chapter 25: Getting Help with Money

Mark Hanna: "The name of the game, moving the money from the client's pocket to your pocket."

Jordan Belfort: "But if you can make your clients money at the same time it's advantageous to everyone, correct?"

Mark Hanna: "No."

– The Wolf of Wall Street (2013)

This book is meant to get you started managing your financial life. But you may not have the desire or confidence to do everything yourself. You may want someone to help you figure things out and keep your impulses in check. Where do you turn for help?

Once you look, financial advice is everywhere. You have financial tele-evangelists on call-in shows. You have personal finance columnists and bloggers. You have an industry of over 300,000 "financial advisors" with an alphabet soup of credentials. You have Nobel-prize winning economists, "millionaires next door," rich and poor dads, and your buddy at the bar. Everyone is dispensing financial advice.

At the end of the day, whoever you turn to, three things matter: competence, incentives, and trust. You should talk to potential advisors and probe on each of these.

Competence

Help is best coming from someone who knows what they are doing. Turns out that selling financial products or calling yourself a "financial advisor" just requires passing some basic licensing exams. The bar is low. So to get a handle on competence, here are some things to look for.

Credentials

Credentials are no guarantee, but at least they tell you somebody spent time studying, passing exams, and getting a minimum level of education and experience. There are dozens of credentials in financial services. Here are some of the most widely recognized:

Financial planning	Certified Financial Planner (CFP®)
	Chartered Financial Analyst (CFA®)
	Chartered Financial Consultant (ChFC®)
Taxes	Certified Public Accountant (CPA)
	Enrolled Agent (EA)
Insurance	Chartered Life Underwriter (CLU®)
Investments	Certified Financial Analyst (CFA®)
Estate Planning	Law Degree (Juris Doctor (JD))

Experience

Experience does not mean an advisor should be old. Still, a twenty-two-year-old will probably have less of it. Experience should be *relevant*. You want a sense that a person has encountered situations similar to yours, has seen different market environments, and can think creatively about your situation. You also want someone who knows their limitations and who will direct you to a specialist if necessary.

Expertise

You may require somebody with specialized knowledge in an area such as estate planning, planning for people with disabilities, retirement planning, or debt counseling. Or who has expertise with clients in your profession or demographic (e.g., race, gender, sexual orientation), all of which bring their own planning challenges.

Investment Track Record

If somebody tells you about how they achieved "superior returns" in the past, ignore it. Even if they have lots of charts and graphs. In fact, be suspicious if this is how they try to show that they are "competent." And don't be drawn in by stories or jargon—more often than not these are just dressed-up sales pitches.

Incentives

Financial help is not free. You should know *how* and *how much* you are paying for what you get. Here are the ways people get paid:

Commissions: A percentage of the transaction. For any transaction recommended to you, find out if the advisor earns a commission, and how much. If they say "Oh, the company pays me the commission" that's a red flag. You may not pay directly, but you pay. Also ask whether they earn any "bonuses," "overrides," or other compensation based on the transaction. Finally, ask whether they will earn "trail commissions," which means some ongoing payments after the initial transaction.

Asset-based fees: A percentage of your account balance. While fees are coming down in the investment industry, 1% of your account balances *every year* is still common. Many advisors who use this model tout being "fee-based." We saw the damage this can do to savings in Chapter 12. Fee-based does not mean low cost.

Fixed fee: This could be a periodic dollar amount, or a one-time fee to prepare a financial plan. Lawyers preparing estate plans often work on this model as well.

Hourly rate: Many lawyers and CPAs work on this basis, and it is increasingly common among financial advisors as well.

Salary and bonus: Advisors working for likes of Fidelity and Vanguard may be paid a salary and bonus. Ask whether their bonus is affected by your financial choices.

Once you understand *how* your prospective financial advisors are paid, do the math and *turn percentages it into dollars*. This makes the cost more real and easier to compare.

Why should you even care about all this gory detail? Two reasons. One, it lets you understand the incentive an advisor has to sell one product versus another. Two, it also tells you something about their trustworthiness. If they are transparent, it means they believe in the value of their service. If they are reticent, maybe you shouldn't open up your financial life to them either.

What about personal finance personalities (like Suze Orman or Dave Ramsey), newspaper columnists, authors, and bloggers. They make money by selling stuff—books, seminars, newspapers, courses, ads. They often endorse specific companies and get paid for it. Odd as it seems, even when you call or write in with a specific question they don't call it financial advice. The reason? The answers you get are generic, considered to be general education or entertainment. You didn't pay to get personal advice.

So it is with this book. It falls into the category of general education. It is not personal advice. To be clear, though, I don't get paid by anyone mentioned in it.

Trust

How do you know you can trust a financial professional? If you've found someone you might hire, it's time do a little research.

Background Check

Make sure there hasn't been any known foul play. Start with a Google search of the individual and their firm to learn about them.

Anyone who provides financial advice or sells securities should be registered with the *Financial Industry Regulatory Authority (FINRA).* Check **brokercheck.finra.org** to see whether there have been any disciplinary actions.

Check the certifying organizations for any professional designations to see whether they are a member in good standing. For example, **AICPA** lists disciplinary actions against CPAs.

Fiduciaries

You should ask a prospective advisor whether they will act as your *fiduciary*. This means they have a legal obligation to put your interests ahead of their own. It may surprise you, but many "financial advisors" are not fiduciaries. Often they are only required to make sure their recommendations are "suitable" or are in your "best interest." Those are lower standards which allow them to favor certain products over others that might better serve your needs. It doesn't mean their recommendations are bad. Indeed, I would view an honest and transparent answer from an advisor who is *not* a fiduciary as a sign of trustworthiness.

Custody

Custody (in this context) refers to safeguarding your money. When you put your money in an account at a large bank or brokerage firm, typically that institution is also the *custodian* of your money. Smaller advisory firms often use these large custodians to hold your money. This is good. Be careful about smaller firms that want custody of your assets themselves.[71]

---

[71] This is what allowed Bernie Madoff to make off with billions of dollars of his clients' money.

Interview

Before signing any agreement or contract with a financial professional have a conversation. Talk about how you will interact (in person, virtually, etc.) and how they get paid (see above). Get a feeling for how you fit in with the rest of their client base. Will you be too small to matter? A big fish in a small pond? Do they seem mostly interested in selling you something as opposed to helping you achieve a goal? Do they listen and answer your questions? Do they have humility?

References

Ask for references and talk to those references. Are they current or former clients? Is the financial professional available when needed? Do they listen to their clients' concerns and understand their needs? Are their recommendations personalized or "off the shelf?" Do they explain recommendations and concepts clearly?

Changing Advisors

Once you have a financial advisor remember that this is a business relationship. It's okay to switch if things don't go as you thought they would or your situation changes. You may decide to do more on your own. Your needs may evolve and require different skills. There may be cheaper alternatives. Be professional and polite, but if you gotta go, you gotta go. That's okay.

Resources

Government and Regulatory Agencies		
FINRA	Check disciplinary background of a broker or financial advisor	**https://brokercheck.finra.org/**

Businesses		
The American College	List with descriptions and details of many financial credentials. The American College sponsors many of the designations	**http://www.designationcheck.com/**
Association of Certified Public Accountants (AICPA)	Search disciplinary actions against CPAs by name	**https://www.aicpa.org/forthepublic/**

Chapter 26: Doing Good with Money

James Farmer: "We do what we have to do so we can do what we want to do."

– The Great Debaters (2007)

Most people want to make the world a better place, and one of the ways to do that is to put our money where our beliefs are. Our power as consumers—where we spend, what we buy—is one way to express our priorities. But there are others.

Charitable Contributions

Charitable giving is the most direct and personal way to use money for causes you care about. Most of us know organizations that are important to us. But what if you want to support an issue and don't know who does good work on it. Or you are asked to donate to a charity that you don't know much about. Marketing materials are always full of touching anecdotes, but not all non-profit organizations are well run. And unfortunately there are also outright scams that try to exploit your generosity.

It is not hard to do a basic check on charities. Look them up on watchdog sites such as **Give.org**, **CharityWatch**, and **Charity Navigator**. These services can also help you identify organizations that support a cause you are interested in.

What about deducting contributions from your income to reduce your tax bill? Possibly. Charitable contributions are deductible *if* you itemize deductions on your tax return.[72] You can deduct donations to tax-exempt (so-called 501(c)(3)) organizations. You can also deduct donations to governments, for example your local police department. Make sure the organization qualifies by asking them or by checking the IRS's **database**.

If you get something of value in return for your donation, that portion is not deductible. The charity needs to tell you the deductible amount. It is best to get a written acknowledgement for your tax records.

You can deduct the value of items you donate, such as used clothes, furniture, even cars. Figuring out that value can be tricky but there are pointers in the tax preparation programs and IRS instructions.

There are a bunch of things you cannot deduct: time you put in as a volunteer for a charity, raffle tickets, and political contributions, among others.

ESG Investing

Do you want your investment dollars to support good business practices and avoid harmful products? Check out *ESG* investing, which tries to favor the stocks and bonds of "good" corporate citizens. ESG stands for environmental, social, and (corporate) governance. You'll also hear terms like socially responsible investing, sustainable investing, and impact investing. These all kind of overlap.

The problem is defining what is "good." What issues matter the most to you? People have different views on workplace practices, diversity, executive pay, carbon emissions, gambling, alcohol sales, weapons and firearms sales, nuclear energy, and fossil fuels, all of which can come under the ESG umbrella.

---

[72] Taxpayers who do not itemize may deduct cash contributions of up to $300 in 2020 and 2021.

Likewise, investment companies have many ways of doing ESG investing. When picking securities, they might ask "How much 'bad' stuff does this company do that might hurt its stock price?" or "How much good is this company doing in the world?" or "How is this company treating their employees and customers?" The answers to these questions are not cut and dried. It is also often not obvious how they are translated into investment choices. When you look at who makes the cut, tech companies often get high marks. (Microsoft is #1 on many lists.) You can see how one organization ranks companies at **Just Capital**.

Serious ESG investing takes a lot of work and adds risk. You need to research companies that fit with your priorities and beliefs. Or pay someone to do it for you. You could end up with just a few dozen to invest in, maybe concentrated in just a handful of industries. This is risky.

In the meantime, if you just want an ESG slant to your investment plan, don't abandon the principles from Chapter 14. Emphasize broad diversification (many securities in a fund) and low expense ratios. Here are some ESG funds you can use instead of regular index funds:

Asset Class	Fund Name	Ticker	Expense Ratio	Investment Approach
U.S. Stocks	Vanguard ESG Stock ETF	**ESGV**	0.12%	Invests in about 1,500 stocks screened for ESG criteria. Excludes companies in the following industries: adult entertainment, alcohol, tobacco, weapons, fossil fuels, gambling, and nuclear power
	iShares ESG MSCI USA ETF	**ESGU**	0.15%	Invests in about 300 U.S. stocks with high ESG ratings from rating company MSCI
	Goldman Sachs JUST U.S. Large Cap Equity ETF	**JUST**	0.20%	Invests in about 500 of the largest U.S. stocks with the best ESG rating in their industry from Just Capital
International Stocks	Vanguard ESG International Stock ETF	**VSGX**	0.17%	Invests in about 4,000 international stocks screened for ESG criteria. Excludes companies in the following industries: adult entertainment, alcohol, tobacco, weapons, fossil fuels, gambling, and nuclear power
U.S. Bonds	iShares ESG U.S. Aggregate Bond ETF	**EAGG**	0.10%	Invests in about 1500 bonds. Similar to the AGG ETF but excludes bonds from companies with low ESG ratings by rating company MSCI

Warning: If you choose to invest in ESG funds, remember that "doing good" with your investments does not assure that your investments will do well.

Resources

Government and Regulatory Agencies		
Internal Revenues Service (IRS)	Database of tax-exempt organizations for which donations are deductible	**https://apps.irs.gov/app/eos/**

Businesses		
Guidestar	Provides access to information and data on non-profit organizations	**https://www.guidestar.org/**
Give.org / BBB Wise Giving Alliance	Affiliated with the Better Business Bureau, accredits non-profits based on various standards	**https://www.give.org/**
Charity Navigator	Independent research company that evaluates and scores charities. Covers many thousands of non-profits	**https://www.charitynavigator.org/**
CharityWatch	Independent research company that grades charities from A+ to F. Covers several hundred non-profits	**https://www.charitywatch.org/**

Chapter 27: Money on Steroids

Jack Singer: "Do you know what a straight flush is? It's like... unbeatable."

Betsy: "'Like unbeatable' is not unbeatable."

– Honeymoon in Vegas (1992)

The surest way to financial success is the most boring: save regularly and invest consistently day in and day out and go about your life. That is the recommendation of this book and so this chapter is entirely optional.

People are people. They are impatient. They want to speed up the process. They start (or restart) saving and try to play catch-up late in life. Or they like the thrill. They want to take a flyer at the chance of buying into the next Amazon or Apple stock. Too often they are misled into believing they can buy an investment that earns high return with low risk.

For these people, Wall Street will happily pull up a chair at the table, comp them a steak dinner, and offer up a variety of gambles. Those gambles often employ *leverage*. Leverage can create fantastic returns. Until it doesn't.[73]

---

[73] See Wikipedia, "Long-Term Capital Management"

Leverage

Leverage is a fancy word for debt. It's a way to supercharge investment gains, but also losses. Look at this example.

Say I want to invest $1,000 in the stock market. I decide to use $1,000 from my brokerage account to buy the Vanguard Total Stock Market ETF (VTI). If the market goes up 20%, I end up with $1,200. If it goes down 20%, I'm left with $800. Win 20% or lose 20%.

What if I take my $1,000 *and* I borrow an additional $1,000 at a 5% interest rate? Now I can buy $2,000 of VTI. Then, when the market goes up 20%, I have $2,400. Once I repay the loan with interest ($1,050), I am left with $1,350. The market went up 20% but I increased my investment by 35%. That's the power of leverage.

Now for the flipside. If the market goes *down* by 20%, my investment drops to $1,600. When I repay the loan with interest, I'm left with just $550 instead of $800. Instead of 20%, I lost 45% of my money. That's the risk of leverage.

Notice that the extra loss due to leverage ($250) is more than the extra gain ($150) because either way I had to pay interest on the money I borrowed. The house (the lender) made $50 regardless of what the market did.

Margin

Okay, so where do I borrow the extra $1,000? It could be anywhere, but Wall Street makes it easy. If I set up my brokerage account as a *margin account,* I can automatically borrow when I buy VTI. In other words, the brokerage company will let me buy $2,000 of VTI even if I only have $1,000 in the account. They will lend me the extra $1,000 "on margin" and charge me interest on it.

How can they do this? By using my shares as *security* for the loan.[74] What this means is that if the price of VTI goes down and drops below a certain level I will get a *margin call*. A margin call requires me to put extra money in my account right away, or the brokerage firm will start selling VTI shares to get their loan back. If I don't have extra cash, a margin call can lock in a loss, or worse, wipe me out.

Options

Another popular way to use leverage is with *options*. Options are so-called *derivative* financial instruments that let you create leverage without explicitly borrowing money. The increased risk and reward are built in.

Options are complicated. There are two basic types: call options and put options. I'll just briefly describe them here. Warning: This is *not* enough information to *do* options trading.

Let's use VTI as an example, as before.[75] Here goes.

If you think the stock market will go up you can buy a *call option* on VTI. This option lets you buy 100 shares of VTI for a set price (called the *strike price*) at any point before some date (the *expiration date*.) The price you pay for this option, also called the option *premium*, will be just a fraction of what 100 VTI shares would cost you. Notice you don't *have to* buy the shares. Hence "option."

Once you own the option, if the price of VTI rises above the strike price, you win. You can then buy the VTI shares for the strike price and sell them at the higher market price for an immediate profit.[76] The profit can be quite large compared with the premium you paid. This is the leverage. On the other hand, if the price of VTI doesn't go

---

[74] Recalling the debt terminology from Chapter 7, the margin loan is *secured* by the VTI shares.

[75] Options can be bought on most large stocks and on many other kinds of assets.

[76] In practice you don't have to put up the money to buy VTI. You can simply sell the option and realize the gain.

up, the option expires worthless and you lose your entire investment (the premium).

So, small initial bet, big potential payoff, or lose your wager. Vegas on Wall Street!

The other basic type of option is a *put option*. It works the same way but lets you *sell* VTI at the strike price. It is a bet that the price of VTI will go *down*, allowing you to buy it cheaply in the market and then immediately sell it at the strike price for a gain.

Short Selling

Short selling is a way to bet on the price of something going down. You profit from the price decline. In investing lingo, you are "short" or you "shorted" an asset. (Conversely, when you invest with the hope that the price will go up, you are "long" or "went long" the asset.)

To understand the mechanics of short selling, let's go back to the VTI ETF. Say I'm convinced the stock market is going down. With a short sale I go to my brokerage firm and borrow some shares of VTI. I promise to return the same number of shares plus some interest in cash. Say I borrow eight shares when the price of each share is $125 (or $1,000 worth). I then take the borrowed shares and sell them for $1,000. The $1,000 goes into my margin account at the brokerage firm as collateral.

Some time later, if the price of a share of VTI later goes down 20% to $100, I buy eight shares for $800 in the market. I hand the shares back to the brokerage firm that lent them to me. I collected $1,000 when I sold the borrowed shares and had to pay only $800 when I returned them, along with some interest, leaving me with a profit of a little less than $200.

Now consider the case where the price of a share of VTI goes up instead. Maybe it goes up 20% to $150. To return the shares I borrowed and sold I would have to pay $1,200 for eight shares. I have a loss of $200. Maybe I wait a little to see if the price comes back down. But instead it goes up further to $175. My loss increases to $400. If the price continues to go up there's no limit to how much I could lose. As my loss goes up, I will get margin calls from the brokerage requiring me to put more cash in the account.

Buyer Beware

Leverage, margin, derivatives, and short selling are sharp knives. Brokerage firms are supposed to make you jump through extra hoops before they will let you loose in the kitchen with them. You need special account approvals to use these techniques. Which is as it should be.

But... Wall Street has found a way to peddle them to inexperienced and even unsuspecting investors. Mutual funds and ETFs can use them as part of their investing strategies. Those funds, in turn, can be sold to almost anyone. The consequences can be dire. The first quarter 2020 bear market wiped out a number of funds and their investors.[77]

If you are tempted to stray from basic index funds to investments that use leverage or short-selling remember that these techniques either 1) increase potential return and increase the risk of loss or 2) decrease risk of loss but also reduce the potential return. Sometimes marketing pitches make it sound like an investment will provide higher returns without increasing risk. Don't believe this.

---

[77] Akane Otani and Sebastian Pellejero, "Bankrupt in Just Two Weeks – Individual Investors Get Burned by Collapse of Complex Securities", The Wall Street Journal, 6/1/2020

Employee Stock Options

Companies often give stock options to employees as pay. These (call) options might have a strike price equal to the company's current stock price and be good for ten years. If the stock price increases over that period, the employee can make a profit by "exercising" the option—buying the stock at strike price and then selling it at the higher market price.

Getting it Done

Forrest Gump: "Lieutenant Dan got me invested in some kind of fruit company. So then I got a call from him, saying, 'We don't have to worry about money no more.' And I said, 'That's good! One less thing.'"

– Forrest Gump (1994)

Did you make it this far in the book? You should be able to ace this simple six-question test. See how you compare to the rest of the country and others in your state. Go to: **https://www.usfinancialcapability.org/quiz.php.**

Above all, I encourage you to *take action*. To that end, the next page has a to-do list, which you can also download from this book's website. Go through it and take charge of your financial life. You may not find the next Apple Computer to invest in, but I hope you too will be able say, one day, "One less thing."

Checklist

		Chapter
☐	Calculate your lifetime income. Undecided career? Check this out	2
	Have a job?	
☐	Review your benefits	3,22
☐	Set up contributions to your 401(k) / 403(b) at least to get company match	3,14
☐	Open or review your checking, savings, and brokerage accounts	4
☐	Are you paying fees for checking? Consider a change	4
☐	Are you earning relatively high interest in an on-line savings account?	4
☐	Have a non-retirement goal more than 5 years out? Open a brokerage account	11
☐	Create a cashflow statement. How close are you to 50-30-20?	5
☐	Create a balance sheet. What is your net worth?	5
☐	Sharing finances with a partner / roommates? Have "the talk"	16
☐	Write down your goals. Be sure to include dollar amounts and timeframes	5
☐	Create a budget with the tool of your choice	5
☐	Automate savings	10
☐	Contributions to retirement plan or IRA	10
☐	Deposits to savings account and/or brokerage account each paycheck	10
☐	Contributions to a 529 Plan	10
☐	Review your debts. Write them down and make a plan to pay them off	7,8,9
☐	Check current interest rates. Decide whether refinancing your debt makes sense	9
☐	Check your credit score	9
☐	Make a plan to (re)build it	9
☐	Freeze your score if not applying for a loan or job	9
☐	Figure out and write down your investment plan	14
☐	Protect yourself against hackers. Set up a password manager and 2FA	23
☐	Review your insurance	21
☐	Disability insurance	21
☐	Life insurance	21
☐	Rental / homeowner / auto / umbrella insurance	22
☐	Make a will. Do it now if you have kids	19

Author

Peter Hofmann has more than thirty years of experience as an insurance and banking executive, investment analyst, and financial planner. A Chartered Financial Analyst®, he regularly volunteers as a financial literacy coach and tax preparer. He lives in Westchester County, New York.

Made in the USA
Monee, IL
04 November 2026

67383592R00108